North Webster

North Webster

A Photographic History of a Black Community

by Ann Morris and Henrietta Ambrose

with photographic restorations by John Nagel

Indiana University Press · BLOOMINGTON & INDIANAPOLIS

The paper used in this publication meets the minimum requirements of American
National Standard for Information Sciences—Permanence of Paper for Printed
Library Materials, ANSI Z39.48-1984.

 ™

Printed in Hong Kong

Library of Congress Cataloging-in-Publication Data

Morris, Ann, date
    North Webster : a photographic history of a Black community / by
Ann Morris and Henrietta Ambrose ; with photographic restorations by
John Nagel.
        p.   cm.
    ISBN 0-253-33895-6. — ISBN 0-253-28601-8 (pbk.)
    1. Afro-Americans—Missouri—Webster Groves—History—Pictorial
works.   2. North Webster (Webster Groves, Mo.)—History—Pictorial
works.   3. Webster Groves (Mo.)—History—Pictorial works.
I. Ambrose, Henrietta.   II. Nagel, John Wm. (John William), date.
III. Title.
F474.W38M67   1993
977.8'65—dc20   93-9619

            1 2 3 4 5   97 96 95 94 93

This book was funded in part by grants from Boatmen's National Bank
of St. Louis and the Richard S. Brownlee Fund of
the State Historical Society of Missouri.

This book is dedicated to Walter Ambrose,
Rosemary Nagel, and Charles Rehkopf, whose support,
encouragement, and help made the book possible; to Doris Wesley,
who typed the manuscript many times; to the many people who
shared their stories and their photographs; and
to our children and all children
who need to understand
the past.

▽

FOREWORD

North Webster is the joyously uplifting story of a people's triumph over tribulation, aversion to adversity, and pride over prejudice. The following pages detail a gloriously positive story which disproves past, present, and future notions that America's black population cannot effectively embrace love, family commitment, religious fervor, industriousness, career advancement, and academic achievement.

Long before the Declaration of Independence, by and for white Americans, historical accounts which are not white-washed reveal that an impressive number of America's non-white, non-citizens displayed a keen interest in all of the above. Those shackled in bondage sometimes showed inexplicable love for the master who kept them enslaved—especially on the death of the latter. Listen to the words of the lament in "Massa's in de Cold, Cold Ground." Slaves grieved at the auction-block sale of loved ones and sometimes spent their full lifetimes after manumission desperately trying to find spouses, relatives, and friends scattered with the winds of insensitivity across a divided nation. Many hundreds of thousands of slaves worshipped a Savior with whom they had little initial familiarity in order to cross the River Jordan into the golden streets of Heaven. Blacks in bondage, like Elizabeth Keckley, saved pennies from side work to buy their freedom. And slaves and freedmen alike plotted and planned, like John Berry Meachum, to violate laws aimed at keeping them from getting a handle on the "Three R's."

These are the exact traits which distinguished and propelled the first black residents of North Webster and their descendants unto this day. They recognized before they arrived in North Webster that true freedom, political and economic advancement, and an ultimate piece of the American dream could come only through a strong family structure, an unshakable belief in that old-time religion, marketable labor skills, and a sound academic underpinning.

The reader will follow with interest this look at the history of black America in microcosm. From the 1804 arrival of the first black slaves in North Webster; through America's wars and depressions and industrial revolution; through the geographical growing pains of this fiercely independent midwestern oasis for blacks; through the social life of a minority community which chose to be endogamous; and through the stark realities of racial equality—earned and expected, but denied—in the 1950s and '60s, the story of North Webster is colorful, enlightening, and uplifting.

The reader need not recognize the names of the cast of characters in the North Webster story, but with a little bit of empathy and imagination the reader will come to know and appreciate the prototypes of a hearty crop of heroic African Americans. They made, are making, and will make the anthem "We Shall Overcome" a promise!

—Julius K. Hunter

Edward Bolden, the Negro, did some axing on the old cottonwood tree that fell this week up at my place. And he told me that he came to Webster Groves in 1865 after he had been mustered out of the Union Army. He was born in Virginia and when ten years old was sold and taken to Mississippi. During the war he escaped to the Union Army and fought at the siege of Vicksburg.

When I asked him which side he fought on, he replied, "Which side do you suppose I fought on? I was sold from Virginia. We were put on the block and sold like any other goods. I never saw my parents afterwards."

"It is horrible," I said.

"Yes," he replied, "they did not treat us right. It makes me rage now whenever I think of it."

Kate Moody
January 13, 1922

This is the story of North Webster, a small black community within an upper-middle-class suburb of St. Louis, Missouri. It tells of the ambiguous relationship between blacks and whites in Missouri, of slavery and freedmen, of segregation and civil rights, of poverty, politics, ambition, and heroes. It is the story of families and churches and an outstanding school, a story in which we find the human potential for perseverance and achievement.

Missouri is the enigma of a border state, both North and South, yet neither one. It was admitted to the Union as a slave state, but its economy was not dependent on slavery, except in the center of the state, where hemp was raised. Business leaders and clergy from New England saw the evils of slavery, sometimes purchasing slaves to manumit them, but seldom debating the issue, wishing instead to avoid conflict by remaining silent. In 1847 Missouri passed a law prohibiting anyone from teaching blacks or mulattoes to read or write. John Berry Meachum, a free black preacher, moved his school to a riverboat in the middle of the Mississippi River where the law did not apply. When the Civil War came, Missouri Governor Claiborne Jackson refused President Lincoln's request for the state militia to fight the Confederates, but in a special convention, Missouri elected to remain in the Union and form a provisional government. When Lincoln emancipated the slaves in 1863 as an act of war, he freed only the slaves in the Confederate states. Missouri did not emancipate its slaves until 1865, when the war was over, just before the Thirteenth Amendment to the Constitution abolished slavery in all the states.

Although Missouri moved quickly after the war to establish schools for blacks, the education of blacks soon became an afterthought, deemed unnecessary beyond the eighth grade. In 1866 the officers and soldiers of the Sixty-second and Sixty-fifth regiments of the United States Colored Infantry raised $6,000 to found Lincoln Institute, a high school and teachers' college for black students in Jefferson City, Missouri. It was the only high school for blacks in the state of Missouri until the St. Louis School Board established Sumner High

School for blacks in 1875. In 1918 the Missouri Supreme Court decided that all school districts which provided a high-school education for whites must provide a separate but equal high-school education for blacks; most districts did so by paying the tuition for their black students to attend high school in the few districts that had black high schools. After the United States Supreme Court ruled, in 1954, that school segregation laws were not legal, it took several years for Missouri school districts to integrate, and many black teachers lost their jobs. The state of Missouri established a Commission on Human Rights in 1957, but until the legislature passed the Missouri Public Accommodations Act of 1965, it was still common practice for Missourians to prohibit blacks from using public facilities—hotels, motels, restaurants, dining rooms, soda fountains, theaters.

Ten miles west of St. Louis, in the town of Webster Groves, where two great hills come together and Shady Creek winds down between them, there is an old black community. It is called North Webster because it covers the hill which rolls to the northern boundary of Webster Groves. For a long time it looked like much of the rural South: rundown, with dirt roads and privies. But it has always been a wonderful place to live, with tall trees to shade the hottest days, creeks full of "crawdads," homegrown vegetables, a good school, and seven churches.

Originally black families moved to North Webster because they could find work with Webster Groves families. Men who had mules and wagons hauled feed, grain, lumber, groceries, and other goods for Webster Groves businesses. Others worked for the railroad, catching the train at the Webster Station. North Webster had an early school, begun right after the Civil War. It became one of the finest schools for blacks in Missouri, attracting black families to the community. The people of North Webster worked together, teaching their children to excel, to aspire, to plan for college. A warm and busy social life was self-contained within the school and the churches. It was only when blacks stepped beyond the hills of North Webster that a veil of discrimination clouded their dreams and slowed the progress of the dreamers.

In 1804, shortly after the Louisiana Purchase, Louis Bompart, a French fur trader, acquired sixteen hundred acres along Manchester Road, north of the area that would become Webster Groves. There is no record of the names of his slaves, but they were probably the first blacks in the area. Slaves made it possible to farm the lonely wooded wilderness. The only other humans around were occasional Indians traveling the trail to the Big Bend in the Meramec River.

In 1832 James and John Marshall and their two sisters came to this area from Virginia, bringing their slaves. James purchased five hundred acres along Manchester Road which is now the town of Rock Hill. John purchased three hundred acres to the south which became North Webster and the Old Webster Business District. The Marshall brothers and their slaves farmed the rolling prairie hills and opened a trading post on Manchester Road.

James Marshall built an elegant two-story frame house next to the trading post in 1840. He named his home Fairfax after Lord Fairfax of Virginia, and it became a stagecoach stop on the route to Kansas City. James married Elizabeth McCausland. They had five children and owned eight slaves. John built a house on Manchester and married Cynthia Berry. They had no children and owned as many as twelve slaves.

In 1845 James Marshall contributed land for the Rock Hill Presbyterian Church. His slaves built the little chapel using stone they quarried from the Fairfax farm quarry. During its construction, Tom White, the overseer, went to Marshall and told him that the slaves wanted to contribute something special to the church. They built the roof on Sundays, on their own time. About twenty-five or thirty slaves attended the Rock Hill Presbyterian Church, always sitting in the back. Some of them came from the Old Orchard area, where large landowners used slaves to farm and work in the orchards.

In 1853 the Pacific Railroad laid tracks and began operating a commuter train through Webster Groves, as far west as Kirkwood. The railroad put a stop at Rock Hill Road and called it Webster, after the Webster College for Boys, which had opened early in 1853. The Reverend Artemus Bullard of St. Louis founded the Webster College for Boys as a Presbyterian college and prep school, bringing educators from New England to teach in the large gray stone building on top of the hill. At first the school prospered, but Bullard died in the Gasconade River train disaster in November 1855, and without his charismatic leadership, the college became a private high school. It closed in 1859 amid the tension of the impending Civil War. The New England educators remained in the Webster Groves area, were active members of the Rock Hill Presbyterian Church, and silently opposed slavery. There is a legend that the college was part of the Underground Railroad, but although the sympathies of the teachers lend credibility to the story, it has never been proved.

Other northern sympathizers moved near the Webster Station, commuting to St. Louis for business. They attended Rock Hill Presbyterian Church because it was still the only church for miles around.

And out of deference to James Marshall, who had built the church, they never discussed slavery on Sunday.

When the war came, things remained quiet in Webster Groves. Even the slave owners supported the Union. Although Lincoln's Emancipation Proclamation in 1863 did not free the slaves in Missouri, James Marshall manumitted his two favorite slaves, John Purnell and Caleb Townsend, before his death in February 1864. He gave Purnell four acres and helped him build a two-story log cabin. Purnell's son, Ed, lived in the primitive old cabin into the 1930s. Marshall gave "Uncle Cape" Townsend four acres on the hill that is now North Webster. After the war, some of Townsend's many children worked as servants for the Marshall family. One of his daughters married a Marshall after moving to Chicago. (Interracial marriages were illegal in Missouri until 1969.)

The United States censuses of 1870 and 1880 show that freed slaves remained in the area, living with their masters, after the war. Cynthia Marshall gave two acres to her freed slave James Winchester, a painter. John Wesley, a laborer, lived with his wife and son at Cynthia Marshall's in 1870. Tom White, the old overseer, was a servant living with Ernest Marshall, James and Elizabeth's son. John Smith, a farmer, and his wife also lived with Ernest Marshall in 1880. These black families probably had their own rustic log cabins on the Marshalls' farms. Black families still lived with large landowners in Old Orchard until well into the 1880s, working as servants and farmhands.

As the dust clouds of the Civil War settled and soldiers returned home, freedmen crossed the country looking for relatives, homes, and jobs. Allen and Julia Brown came from Alabama with a wagon and a mule given them by their former master. Initially the Browns settled by Shady Creek where the land was low and flat, but the creek flooded, so they moved to William Porter's subdivision.

Porter was a retired Congregational minister living in Webster Groves. In 1866 he bought land behind Henry Prehn's store on North Gore and subdivided it into small lots for freedmen who wanted to build their own homes. Porter's subdivision ran from Pacific Avenue down the steep side of the hill through the woods to Shady Creek and Shady Avenue. At the bottom of the hill Porter helped the black families build a church. At the top of the hill he named the streets Lincoln and Sherman.

Allen Brown built a little frame house on the corner of Lincoln and Sherman. He used his wagon to haul grain for Henry Prehn's Grocery, and later for Henry Schulz's Feed Company, picking up the grain in East St. Louis and sometimes driving across the Mississippi River when it was frozen solid. Brown's youngest son, George, ran away from home when he was still a boy and fought in the Spanish-American War. Brown's oldest son, Arnold, built a house next to his father's in the subdivision he called "Vinegar Hill."

Other black families built cabins on Vinegar Hill and along Shady Creek, including Augustus Toliver, William Wright, Henry Jackson, Alexander Fletcher, Jackson Carr, Lee Bowman, Edward Bolden, and Ken Lankford. They were all farm laborers except Lankford, who was a preacher.

Lankford preached at the First Baptist Church of Webster Groves, which began meeting in a brush arbor under the trees by Shady Creek right after the war. William Porter helped to organize it formally in 1866, the same year that the First Congregational, Emmanuel Episcopal, and Webster Groves Presbyterian, the oldest churches in Webster Groves, were established. Allen Brown contributed the first twenty-five dollars for the church, which had nineteen original members. They built a small frame building with a high foundation, because it was next to the creek. Their singing and shouting resounded down the dusty road, lifting spirits and giving black families a sense of community.

Emanuel Cartwright also preached at the First Baptist Church. He built a house nearby on Shady Avenue in 1869. He had worked in St. Louis with John Berry Meachum, the black preacher and teacher, before the Civil War. Cartwright became the preacher of the African Baptist Church when Meachum died in 1854, and he took over Meachum's riverboat school for blacks on the Mississippi. Besides preaching in Webster Groves, Cartwright organized the Rose Hill Baptist Church in Kirkwood and led the Union Baptist Association, an association of black Baptist churches in eastern Missouri.

Across the dusty road from Cartwright and the First Baptist Church lived Charles and Hester Foster and their five children. Charles worked as a day laborer for Edward Jackson, and Hester took in washing for the wealthiest families in Webster. According to Tom Gibson, who grew up in Webster at the turn of the century, Hester was really "Somebody." A large woman with a deep laugh, she wore many petticoats and smelled of Creole cooking. She planted her long front hill in flowers that bloomed all summer, warning children not to pick her flowers or she would put a curse on them. Hester had a grand barbecue every year and invited the white families for whom she did washing. It was the most important social event in Webster Groves, with paper lanterns strung from the trees and an air of Creole mystery.

In 1866, the year the First Baptist Church was organized, an Englishwoman named Mrs. Dotwell came through Webster Groves on a mission to establish schools for blacks throughout Missouri. Working for James Milton Turner, assistant state superintendent of public schools in charge of postwar Negro schools, she began teaching black children in the church. In the early years, classes stopped during the month of October so the children could help with the harvest.

Two years later, in 1868, the School District of Webster Groves was established and took over the responsibility of the little school for blacks. Emma Babcock donated her teaching services, and the school board paid her carfare. There were thirty black children eligible for school between the ages of five and twenty-one, eighteen boys and twelve girls.

T. A. Bush became the first Negro teacher of the school in 1871. He taught twenty-three pupils in the little church during the day, and the school board provided him with extra coal for his evening school. But soon the board suspected that the church was using coal intended for the school, and in 1872 the district built a separate one-room log school just west of the First Baptist Church on Shady Avenue. The teachers for the next six school years were Lottie Martling, Jennie Swayne, Perry Molatt, Lottie Martling (again), Ann A. Hadley, and Mary A. Clancey.

Beginning in 1878, Jeannette Davis taught in the little log school-house for five years. She lived with Augustus Toliver's family on Vinegar Hill and attended the white Congregational Church until she left Webster Groves, in 1883, to found a girls' school in Mount Coffee, Liberia. She came back to Webster Groves several times to raise money for the school.

Black families moved from rural areas of the South to settle along Shady Avenue near the creek, the school, and the church. They could find work with Webster families as gardeners, handymen, laundresses, and cooks, or as teamsters for local businesses. Anderson Morrison, a teamster, and his wife, Anna, came to Webster Groves from Searcy, Arkansas, around 1870. They had three children. Anna died soon after their baby, Theodore, was born, and the Morrisons' neighbors, Philip and Lucy Grice, raised Theodore as if he were their own child. Grice had a farm on Shady Avenue and sold groceries.

Abe and Nancy Givens and their three children came to Webster Groves from Kentucky in the 1870s. Givens owned a small farm on Slocum Avenue and did day labor. Burl Burnett brought his wife, Agnes, his mother, and two children to North Webster in the 1870s. Burnett worked for Edwin Tichnor, a Webster contractor, for forty-two years. A familiar sight at the turn of the century was old Mr. Tichnor, with his Vandyke beard, flowing cape, and cane, strolling through

Webster Groves with his sidekick, Burnett, discussing where they would build their next new house. Agnes Burnett instilled in her children a philosophy that other families in North Webster shared: "Never work for poor white trash. You don't learn anything from them." Blacks in Webster Groves wanted to get ahead.

The censuses show that some black families were very young. In 1880 Harvey and Etta Simms lived on Shady Avenue. Harvey was twenty-one and Etta was nineteen years old. Jacob Esaw was also living in North Webster by then. He was twenty-one, and his wife, Maria, was only seventeen. Esaw had met his young wife in Searcy, Arkansas, when he was working for the railroad. Jacob weighed about 225 pounds. Maria, a small, beautiful woman, had hair down to her waist and was of French and Indian blood. Esaw worked for Ed Hart, the third mayor of Webster Groves, who owned a printing company in St. Louis. The two men commuted on the train every day. Esaw rode in a separate car.

In 1884 the Reverend J. B. Bunch started the African Methodist Episcopal Zion Mission Church in Webster Groves. The church met in a wooden storefront at Gore and Moody, near the train station. Bishop G. L. Blackwell took over, and in 1889 the members voted to name their church Blackwell Chapel A.M.E. Zion. In 1891 the congregation raised its own frame building on Shady Avenue near the First Baptist Church. Then in 1916 Blackwell Chapel built the present stone building on the hill on North Elm Avenue. On Sunday, September 3, 1916, the men, women, and children of Blackwell Chapel, including Esaws, Givenses, and Morrisons, marched from their church on Shady to their new church on North Elm, singing "We Are Marching to Zion." On June 1, 1919, they held a "Basket Meeting" picnic to celebrate the burning of the mortgage.

Family considerations brought people to North Webster in the 1890s. Charles St. James bought two acres on Holland Avenue in North Webster in 1891, to be near his father-in-law, F. S. K. Taylor. St. James, the son of a Frenchman, had sharecropped on President Ulysses S. Grant's farm in South St. Louis County after the war. After moving to North Webster, he worked as a janitor at the St. Louis County Courthouse in Clayton and continued to buy land in North Webster. By the time his six children grew up, he owned enough land on the top of the hill to build a house for each of them.

In 1893 Albert D. Pierson came with his wife and six children from Virginia to be near his brother. Before the war his brother had belonged to the Lucases, a prominent French family in St. Louis. Both brothers lived on Vinegar Hill. Albert Pierson became the janitor of the

Webster Groves City Hall and post office and later built septic tanks for the city.

Frank Stone moved his family to North Webster from Franklin County, Missouri, in 1893, so that his children could get a better education. He had eleven daughters and one son.

By the 1890s, between seventy-five and ninety pupils attended school in the one-room log cabin on Shady Avenue. Richard A. Hudlin managed all those children by himself from 1890 through 1892. During his tenure the school burned to the ground, and classes moved back to the First Baptist Church. In the early part of 1892, the church burned, and the church and school moved to the storefront at Gore and Moody vacated by Blackwell Chapel. Because of the fires, the Webster Groves School Board built a two-room frame schoolhouse on Holland Avenue near the ravine. John A. Agee became the first principal, also teaching the older students, and Lulu Farmer was appointed as his assistant to teach the younger children.

In 1895, parents from North Webster met with the school board to ask that their school be given a name. The board decided that the students should submit names, from which one would be selected. The children suggested the names of many famous men, but Frederick Douglass was the only Negro among them.

Frederick Douglass had escaped from slavery, and during the 1840s he became famous as an antislavery orator. He published the *North Star,* an abolitionist newspaper, supported women's rights and the Underground Railroad, recruited Negroes for the Union Army, and served as United States minister to Haiti. He also attended Abraham Lincoln's inauguration reception. His name was a logical, inspiring choice.

In September 1895, Lulu Farmer became the principal of Douglass School. Arrena Brown taught the younger children. Mary Brown, Arnold Brown, and Theodore Morrison were the first students to graduate from the eighth grade, in 1898. That first graduation ceremony took place at the First Baptist Church on Monday, June 6, at 8:00 P.M.

At the turn of the century, Douglass School was rustic, a little two-room country school. Neither Douglass nor Webster School (for whites) had running water or electricity. In the winter Douglass was heated by a stove. Both rooms had a bucket of water from the cistern, and the children brought their own tin cups, or had to drink out of the dipper. Two latrines stood in the yard, one for the boys and one for the girls. The boys and the girls played separately on the playground. The girls played hopscotch and jumped rope. The boys played marbles and soccer. Girls played softball with girls, and boys played softball with boys.

Fields covered the hills of North Webster. The dirt roads became so muddy in the spring that children wore boots. Grass grew tall in the summer, full of wildflowers. A dense growth of trees shaded the hill along Shady Creek, giving the creek and Shady Avenue their names. Near the woods along Deer Creek, to the north, three deep spring-fed ponds dotted the landscape: one at Cornell and Wellington, one at Thornton and Bell, and one at Bell and Alementor. Beautiful white and lavender water lilies bloomed on the surface of the water in the summer. Bullfrogs hid in the cattails around the ponds, and in the spring, peepers sang at dusk as the stars came out. A larger pond sparkled in the sun west of Rock Hill Road. Boys caught big catfish in all the ponds.

Families in North Webster planted vegetable gardens and fruit trees, and many families raised chickens, hogs, and a cow or two. Neighbors exchanged tools and helped each other with hog killing in November. Dinner might include home-grown greens, beans, corn, peas, squash, carrots, sweet potatoes, or tomatoes. Children who grew up on homemade biscuits and cornbread with homemade applebutter longed for store-bought bread. On Sundays families cooked the "Holy Bird" (fried chicken), in case the preacher came to dinner.

Children had many chores. Every day before school, Harold Esaw milked the Warrens' cow and carried milk to the minister's family at Emmanuel Episcopal Church, over a mile away. After school, Luther St. James carried water from the spring at the bottom of the hill on Shady Creek up to his house for his mother. Then he moved the stake to which the cow was tied so that she could reach fresh grass and shade. Many of the women in North Webster took in washing, and the children delivered the clean clothes after school.

In the summer, children caught bucketfuls of crawdads in the creek. Their mothers boiled the crawdads and served them with melted butter. The boys loved to swim in a deep swimming hole where Shady Creek flowed into Deer Creek, but the girls stayed away because the boys might be skinny-dipping.

Winters were cold, and much snow covered the ground. Children sledded down Elm, Ravine, and Holland. Boys made bobsleds and flew down the big hill behind the St. James house, rolling off the sleds just in time to avoid plunging into the creek.

Members of the St. James family remember the magic winter nights when all nine of them, including their grandmother, sat around the kitchen table, their plates filled from a big pot of beans on the stove, and their daddy told them they could go ice skating after supper. Charles St. James loaded a wheelbarrow with firewood, lit a coal-oil

9

lantern, and led the way through the snow, over the hill, to the big pond at Rock Hill Road and Bismark, where he built a bonfire. Others came, blacks and whites, and they all skated. The best skater by far was Charles St. James. He even liked to skate on Deer Creek. One night he was skating on the creek by himself and fell through the ice, and when he got home he was stiff and covered with icicles.

The year 1902 was the first year that eighth-grade graduates from Douglass went on to Sumner High School in St. Louis. All seven of them went: Eleanor Brown, Romeo Burnett, Leticia Cole, Joe Hunter, Lula Morrison, Ethel Stone, and her sister, Josephine Stone. They rode the train into Union Station at eight o'clock in the morning, then walked the three blocks to Sumner. At that time Sumner was located at 15th and Walnut, where Kiel Auditorium is now.

Sumner was founded in 1875 and named for Charles Sumner, the United States senator from Massachusetts who was ardent in his opposition to slavery. In northern states black children attended the same public schools as white children, but the constitutions of southern states, including Missouri, required separate schools for blacks. An act of Congress established Dunbar High School for blacks in Washington, D.C., in 1870. It had trustees and a special admissions policy. St. Louis was the first public school district to provide a black high school, and it included a teacher-training department.

The principal of Sumner High School for the first four years was a white man named Alvah Clayton, who lived in Webster Groves. After Clayton, all of the principals and teachers at Sumner were black. They were some of the finest high-school teachers in the country, for there were few opportunities at the time for black intellectuals with advanced degrees, except at black universities in the South, Dunbar High School in Washington, D.C., or Sumner High School in St. Louis. Dr. Edward Bouchet is a good example of the quality of the Sumner faculty. He was the first Negro to receive a Ph.D., and the first black member of Phi Beta Kappa. Bouchet received his Ph.D. in physics from Yale University in 1876 and taught at Sumner High School at the turn of the century. Because Sumner recruited great intellectuals, it became a paragon of excellence. Many families from the South made special arrangements for their children to live in St. Louis so they could attend Sumner High School.

Lincoln Nelson was the principal of Douglass School in 1903. He established a self-improvement club, which met on Tuesday evenings to hear a speaker, often a minister from a white church, and to circulate magazines and books from the Congregational Church reading room. In 1904 Professor Thomas A. Moore became the principal. A tall man, dignified and strict, he taught seventh and eighth grade and served as principal for twenty-one years. His students remember him as a great math teacher.

Professor Moore's first year at Douglass was also the year of the St. Louis World's Fair. Theodore Morrison worked at the fairgrounds, riding the Kirkwood-Ferguson streetcar in from North Webster every day that summer. He met his wife, Maggie, who was visiting from Pulaski, Tennessee, at the fair. Many black families from the rural South came to St. Louis for the first time to visit the World's Fair. The job opportunities and the excitement of the big city enchanted the visitors, and many decided to move to St. Louis. They stayed with relatives or at boarding houses near Union Station. Perhaps a traveler or two stayed at Annie Polk's house in North Webster, riding the trolley in to the fair. Annie Polk came to Webster as a slave, and sometime after the war her master gave her land on Euclid Avenue, where she built her home. Occasionally, at the turn of the century, she rented rooms. Usually her boarders were teachers from Douglass.

As North Webster grew, churches and a Masonic Lodge sprang up. In the fall of 1908, the Reverend B. F. Abbott held a spiritual revival in a tent in an open field on Cornell Avenue. His stirring evangelism led to the organization of the Webster Groves Methodist Episcopal Church. The Reverend C. C. Kitchen was the first pastor. In 1911 the congregation built a permanent church across the street on the west side of Cornell Avenue.

Sometime before 1910, the Masonic Lodge of North Webster built Pointer's Hall on the east side of Shady Avenue where Shady Creek wound close around behind it. They named it for one of their members, and it became an ageless landmark, tall and weather-beaten, dark and mysterious. It had living quarters on the first floor and a large meeting hall on the second floor. According to their charter, the Masons of North Webster organized Morning Star Lodge #92 on August 20, 1880. The Masons met upstairs in Pointer's Hall, and so did their wives, the Eastern Stars. The Masons were an important part of most ceremonies in North Webster. They laid the cornerstone for each new church building, gave speeches, and performed rituals at most funerals, to the dismay of restless children. They also distributed baskets of food at Thanksgiving and Christmas to poor families in North Webster. The Eastern Stars were a warm, supportive group of women, helping each other in times of sickness or hardship with cooking, housekeeping, and small loans.

Trauma threatened the members of the First Baptist Church of Webster Groves in 1913. White folks in the Tuxedo Park neighborhood organized a Baptist church and wanted to name it First Baptist Church of Webster Groves. People in the black community were afraid that the white congregation would succeed in expropriating the name of their forty-seven-year-old church. As a young girl, Della St. James heard her mother cry about it in the night. But the First Baptist Church of Webster Groves had legally incorporated in the state of Missouri in the 1880s, and the name was irrevocably theirs. The church in Tuxedo Park became the Webster Groves Baptist Church.

In 1915 people who had belonged to A.M.E. churches before moving to North Webster decided to organize one in their new community. They met at Peter Elkins's house on June 17 to organize the Union Mission Church. Theodore Morrison served as the first pastor. Because his family kept growing, the Reverend Morrison always had two jobs: he worked as a clerk in the St. Louis County Recorder of Deeds Office in addition to preaching. At first the Union Mission Church met in Pointer's Hall. Around 1919 the members purchased the old A.M.E. Zion church on Shady Avenue near Lincoln Avenue, renaming it Parks Chapel in honor of the late Bishop Henry Blanton Parks. The membership of Parks Chapel continued to grow. In 1927 they erected a building on East Avenue, in 1930 they built a bigger church on Tuxedo Avenue, and today they have a beautiful brick church next to the former YMCA on Holland Avenue.

Between 1917 and 1918, the stirring gospel music of the Sanctified Church of God in Christ began echoing over the hills of North Webster and floating in through the open windows of homes as far away as Tuxedo Park. On hot summer nights people listened from their front porches, and children drifted off to sleep to the haunting rhythms of heartfelt spirituals accompanied by guitars, tambourines, and an old piano.

Before that time, families had ridden the streetcar to the Reverend Bostick's Sanctified Church of God in Christ at 23rd and Morgan Street (now Delmar Boulevard) in St. Louis. Sometimes the Reverend Bostick and his wife came out to North Webster to meet with families in their homes. During World War I, those families organized the Sanctified Church of God in Christ in Webster Groves and held services in Latolee Simms's side yard, with Louis Metcalf as the first pastor. The church met for a while in a tar-paper shack on Taylor (now Thornton) at Bell, across from the lily pond. The guitars and tambourines filled the little shack with music so that the congregation inside forgot where they were. Finally, in 1928 the congregation built a frame church on Thornton, and almost fifty years later they remodeled it in brick. The stirring gospel music still echoes across the hills on prayer nights.

As families added to the spiritual life of North Webster, they also enhanced its intellectual atmosphere. During the summer of 1913, Charles St. James and some other men dug a basement under Douglass School. Luther St. James was a little boy then, and he remembers carrying water from the spring for his father and the other workers. The basement became the classroom for the first, second, and third grades. Susie Crockett taught the younger students in the "Rat Hole," instilling in them a fine philosophy by having them memorize the 23rd Psalm and passages from Shakespeare, such as "This above all, to thine own-self be true. . . . "

In the fall of 1915, Frank Stone and other residents of North Webster went to the school board and requested a high school for their children. The board did not honor their request, but instead hired a fourth teacher. High-school classes had begun for white children in Webster Groves in 1897, and a high-school building for whites had been built in 1906.

In 1916, Douglass School was wired for electricity, and Harvey Simms joined the faculty. Simms had graduated from Douglass in 1906 and attended Lincoln Institute in Jefferson City, Missouri. A small man who walked with a crutch, he taught fifth and sixth grades, sometimes delighting his students with a taffy pull. He played football, coached baseball, and organized the first Douglass School Band. He directed the band for ten years, and some of its members later became professional musicians. Joe Thomas, one of his students, went on to play with Duke Ellington.

Enrollment at Douglass School reached 108, and still there was no provision for a high-school education for the black youth of Webster Groves. Tuition at Sumner High School in St. Louis was a hundred dollars, and with fathers in North Webster earning fifty cents a day, tuition and train fare were beyond the means of most families in the community.

In 1917 Frank Stone and Augustus Ewing from Webster Groves and Mr. and Mrs. William H. Jenkins from Kirkwood hired a lawyer and went to Jefferson City to demand a free high-school education for their children and for all black children in Missouri. Finally, in 1918, the Supreme Court of Missouri ruled that education must be separate but equal. Any school district with a high school for white students had to make provisions to educate its black students. In June 1918, the Webster Groves Board of Education agreed to pay seventy-five dollars toward the tuition of each student who attended Sumner High School.

In 1919 four Webster Groves students attended Sumner, and the school board records indicate that it paid only $120 in tuition for all four students. That year Luther St. James was the only eighth-grader to graduate from Douglass School. Older boys had gone to war.

Twenty-nine young men from North Webster enlisted during World War I: William Bowen, Edward Bowman, John Brooks, Wesley Buril, William Collins, Benjamin Conway, William Davis, Giles Esaw, Robert Farrell, Russell Givens, Donald Inge, Robert James, Sylvester James, Raymond Jones, Frank Lyles, John Monroe, William Morgan, George Morrison, Herbert Redmond, Henry Renfro, John Rhodes, Joseph Rhodes, David Smith, Hugh Stone, Herbert Thomas, Philip Thomas, Henry Turner, Jesse Williams, and Jesse Wright. The armed forces were segregated during World War I, and black soldiers from the Midwest trained at Camp Funston in Fort Riley, Kansas. They formed the Ninety-second Division of the Second American Army, which went over intact to the Marbache sector of France. The Germans called the Ninety-second the "Black Devils."

When the men came home in 1919, the *St. Louis Post-Dispatch* published a glowing article in the Sunday paper on February 16 called "What Our Negro Soldiers Did in the Great War." All the black soldiers from North Webster marched together in the Webster Groves Memorial Day Parade, from Gore Avenue down Lockwood, Bompart, Newport, and Big Bend, to the memorial celebration and dedication of the giant American flag in the triangular park between Lockwood and Big Bend in Old Orchard. It seemed as if blacks finally were being recognized as equals after their valiant contribution during the Great War.

But the 1920s brought more discrimination. A building boom in Webster Groves in the 1920s led real-estate men to put pressure on black families who lived in other parts of Webster Groves to sell their homes and move to North Webster.

St. Louis and East St. Louis had experienced terrible racial problems during the war. In 1916 the city of St. Louis passed a segregation ordinance which decreed that no person of any race could move to a block where 75 percent of the residents were of another race. The NAACP, founded in 1910 under the leadership of W. E. B. Du Bois, got an injunction against the enforcement of the ordinance, and in 1918 the U.S. Supreme Court declared segregation ordinances unconstitutional.

In addition to the bitter feelings created by the segregation ordinance, the most violent race riot in our country's history broke out in East St. Louis, Illinois, in the summer of 1917. Large companies in East St. Louis, such as the Aluminum Ore Company and the Krey Meat Packing Company, paid very low wages. In order to break the strikes of their union workers, the companies recruited poor black workers from the rural South. This created extreme racial tension, which exploded on July 2, 1917. Whites, including the police and the National Guard, beat and shot hundreds of black men and women and burned their homes; the night was filled with screams and smoke and a terrible orange glow. Black families fled across the Mississippi River, over the Eads Bridge, and in overcrowded ferry boats, laden with all of their possessions, like refugees from the Great War. Many of the refugees never returned to East St. Louis.

Ten miles west of St. Louis, residents of Webster Groves and North Webster only read about the segregation ordinance and the East St. Louis race riot in the newspapers. There was no need for a segregation ordinance in Webster Groves because most Webster Groves deeds had restrictive clauses forbidding the sale of land to Negroes.

As part of a city beautification plan in 1926, the Webster Groves Plan Commission and the Board of Aldermen proposed a bond issue for playgrounds, wider streets, better drainage and sewers, an improved water supply, adequate fire protection, parks, and modern streetlights. The plan called for the condemnation of the churches and all of the houses on Shady Avenue, to create the first Webster Groves city park.

Harvey Simms, who lived on Shady Avenue with his mother, wrote an eloquent letter to the editor of the *Webster News-Times*, printed on March 12, 1926:

We, the Negroes of Shady Avenue, residents of Webster Groves, Missouri, are in favor of the advancements of Webster Groves, Missouri, as well as all of her improvements in every respect, because we realize and believe, as you, that it is impossible for Webster to maintain her high standing as the Queen of the Suburbs, and cease to make striking improvements along all lines.

We are in harmony with the wise and judicious foresightedness of The Citizens' Bond Issue Committee. . . . We highly endorse the movement for Play Grounds, because we believe, as you, that the child's future depends to a very large degree on his being well developed mentally, morally as well as physically. To us it would be a source of never ceasing pleasure to see Webster with beautiful and attractive Park-Ways and Boulevards. . . .

But on the other hand, if these striking improvements are to be made at the expense of our homes, regardless as to how humble they may seem, yet to us they are very dear, because they represent years of honest toil and labor as well as sacrifice. . . .

The Negroes in Webster are peculiarly situated and handicapped somewhat, because we are not allowed or permitted to purchase property and live in all parts of Webster. . . .

If the Park-Ways and Boulevards are made this will deprive at least 100 families of their homes. Hence this move which we do not deem wise to make at this time, will cause our city, churches and schools to suffer, because our families will be compelled to leave Webster. . . .

If these striking and astounding improvements will be made at the expense of our homes, we cannot welcome the movement very willingly and cheerfully, like we would desire to do.

Therefore we, the Negro residents of Shady Avenue, are using this method to appeal to the fair minded and honest voters, to ask you to give our side of the question your undivided consideration and support.

> Yours in distress
> The Shady Avenue Residents
> H. J. Simms.

That single voice with the courage to question the plan of the city fathers helped the residents of Webster Groves to realize the error of beautification at the expense of families. The bond issue failed.

Thus it is no wonder that in the 1920s the philosophy of Marcus Garvey was popular with some of the men in North Webster. Garvey had moved to Harlem from Jamaica in 1916. He was a brilliant speaker, able to articulate the postwar disenchantment of blacks, especially following the race riots in East St. Louis in 1917 and in many other cities in 1919. He organized the United Negro Improvement Association around the philosophies that Negroes must restore their self-respect through pride in a glorious past, they must ensure a promising future by creating Negro-owned enterprises, and they must look to Africa as their once and future homeland. Garvey published a militant weekly newspaper called the *Negro World*.

A group of North Webster men met every Sunday afternoon in the upstairs meeting room of Pointer's Hall, on Shady Avenue across from Ravine Avenue, to read and discuss Garvey's ideas from the *Negro World*. Garvey's followers had a sense of racial pride, and although a back-to-Africa movement never materialized, the North Webster men were eager to support some black-owned businesses.

The first black businesses in North Webster were two grocery stores which came to Webster Groves during the last years of World War I. Realizing that there was no black grocery store in the community, Wesley Webster moved to Webster Groves with his wife, Adelaide, and opened a store on Shady Avenue, two doors west of Pointer's Hall, around 1917 or 1918. Originally from Birmingham, Alabama, Webster had been recruited by a white man to work in a mine in Cape Girardeau, Missouri. But working conditions in the mine were so wretched and the pay was so low that Webster and his family fled to St. Louis, and then to Webster Groves. To supply the little store, Webster drove his horse and wagon into the city every week to pick up his merchandise. Webster died in 1929, and Adelaide Webster sold the store.

Charles Thomas opened the other black-owned grocery, on North Elm, a short time after Webster opened his store. Thomas's parents, Andrew and Miriam, had moved to North Webster from St. Louis in 1915. Andrew Thomas commuted to work at the Peckham Candy Company in St. Louis every day and back every night to his country home. There fruit trees, a vegetable garden, a grape arbor, and a bubbling creek restored his soul. Andrew and Miriam Thomas convinced their sons to move to North Webster, and Charles purchased the neighborhood grocery on North Elm from Mr. Keifer, a white man who had run the store for several years. Charles Thomas's grocery became a North Webster institution. His wife, Alby, and their nine children all helped with the business, and they knew everybody in North Webster. Lots of children stopped at Thomas's Grocery Store on their way home from school to buy penny candy and dill pickles with peppermint sticks in them. Mr. Thomas helped many families through the Depression by extending credit. He added a dry-cleaning business next door and operated both businesses for over forty years.

The typical neighborhood grocery store, like Thomas's and Webster's, was small and rather cluttered, with dark wood floors. It was warm and cozy in the winter and cool in the summer, with a screen door that creaked open and then banged shut. It sold canned goods, flour, cornmeal, sugar, spices, milk, eggs, meat, fresh vegetables, bread, and coffee that was ground at the store. It sold coal oil for kerosene lamps, Ball jars for canning, school supplies, and penny candy. The proprietor waited on each customer, retrieving the merchandise from behind the counter.

White families ran the other neighborhood groceries in North Webster. Schaeffer's, at the corner of Lithia and Plateau, and Tappel's, on Euclid, both opened in the 1920s and lasted until the late 1960s. Harold Schaeffer came to North Webster in 1924 to take over his aunt's corner grocery store. She had opened a dry-goods store between 1910 and 1920, but she was caught selling bootleg whiskey and had to sell the store. The area around Schaeffer's Store, near the Sanctified Church of God in Christ and the lily pond at the top of the hill, was dotted with farmhouses, vegetable gardens, fields, and woods. It was integrated, and all the children played together, not knowing there were differences between them until they realized that they went to different schools.

The Tappels came to North Webster in 1928 and bought a little one-story brick store on Euclid Avenue from the Dubas. The Tappels lived in the back of the store with their two sons; Mrs. Tappel ran the store, while Mr. Tappel worked as a salesman for a wholesale coffee company.

Jim's Market and the Howe Brothers Grocery Store stood on Shady Avenue along the streetcar line in the 1930s and 1940s. A Greek named Jim Magafas ran Jim's Market on the corner of Marshall and Shady where the streetcar stopped before crossing the Deer Creek trestle. Ira and Bill Howe operated their grocery store on the corner of Tuxedo Avenue and Shady and had a gas pump out in front. The Howes also had one of the first telephones in the area, and people dropped by to get telephone messages.

Except for those four businesses owned by whites and two later filling stations near Jim's Market, all the other businesses in North Webster were owned by blacks. In 1920 Preston and Eleanor Rogers opened an ice cream parlor next to their farm on North Elm. Their property ran all the way through to the Douglass School playground. They built a dance pavilion in the back of the ice cream parlor, and on the north side they created a park with tables and benches in the clover. On special holidays, such as the Fourth of July, Preston Rogers hired a dance band and sold barbecued ribs and chicken dinners.

Black families from all over St. Louis came to Abernathy Park in the woods on Bismark Avenue, just west of North Webster. On summer weekends young people and families rode the streetcar out from the hot city, got off at Gore Avenue, and walked up Rockhill Road to Bismark Avenue and Abernathy Park. Picnic tables and a concession stand selling barbecued ribs, soft drinks, and confections stood in the shade of the tall trees. The spring-fed creek running through the park was dammed to make a swimming hole. But the real attraction was the covered, open-air dance pavilion with a live band. On summer nights the music and the lights of the pavilion filled the woods and mixed with the hum of the cicadas to make people forget how hot it was. Late at night, tired, happy people walked back to the streetcar, which ran until midnight into the city.

Mosby Collins opened a barbershop on Shady Avenue, just east of Pointer's Hall, in the early 1920s, and it soon became a gathering place for the men of North Webster. Irene Mitchell graduated from Madam C. J. Walker's School of Beauty Culture on Market Street in St. Louis and taught her little sister, Ruby, to style hair. Then, while Irene worked in St. Louis, Ruby styled ladies' hair in a little building owned by William Winston near Collins's Barber Shop in the 1930s and early

1940s. Lee Moss worked for Mosby Collins for many years, and when incorporation and redevelopment condemned this North Webster institution in 1960, Moss took over the business and moved it across the street to Kirkham Square.

In 1923 Jones C. Lewis came to North Webster and opened an undertaking establishment at Elm and Ravine avenues. Later he moved the business to his home on Euclid Avenue. Before he arrived, blacks held wakes at home, and Louis Bopp from Kirkwood buried the dead. Lewis had worked for Bopp, and Bopp helped him get started. The Reverend Theodore Morrison helped Lewis as a funeral director and public-relations man. They arranged for wakes and funeral services at local churches, as well as at homes, and conducted burials at the Father Dickson Cemetery. Lewis married Susie Crockett, the teacher of the younger students at Douglass School. Ted Yandell, Sr. apprenticed under J. C. Lewis, and when Lewis died in 1948, Susie Lewis made Yandell the funeral director. Yandell's son, Ted Yandell, Jr., owns the business today and conducts most funerals for North Webster, like his father and J. C. Lewis before him.

In the mid-twenties, Herbert Witt bought a large vacant lot at the top of Bell Avenue. He built a house on half the lot and showed outdoor movies at the Sky Dome on the other half. He set up benches in the grass, and his wife, Lucy, sold homemade ice cream, soda pop, and confections to the moviegoers. Witt was a foundry worker. He studied the electrical trade at night, becoming the first black licensed electrician in St. Louis County. The Witts had seven children and always did things together. Herbert Witt played the slide trombone in the African Methodist Church orchestra until he converted to Catholicism in 1930. The Witts held catechism classes in their home, open to anyone in the black community. Black Catholics attended St. Mary Magdalen Catholic Church in Brentwood because they were not welcome at Holy Redeemer Catholic Church in Webster Groves.

Another important series of church events began in 1923 when the First Baptist Church of Webster Groves purchased land for a new building northeast of the old building on Shady Avenue. That same year Roscoe James moved to North Webster from a farm in Union, Missouri, with his wife and two children. He went into the plastering and contracting business with his brother, and for his first big project he built the new First Baptist Church, contributing his own labor for free. Members attended their first service in the new building on Easter Sunday in 1927.

Some members of First Baptist Church could not bear to leave the old building, so for years there were two First Baptist churches in Webster Groves. Finally a lawsuit determined that the Reverend Lee's congregation in the new building was legally the First Baptist Church because they had taken the charter with them. Under the leadership of the Reverend William Catlin, the little group in the old building endeavored to heal the wounds in the community, changing their name in 1945 to the Old Community Baptist Church. Old Community Baptist Church is still on the original site of its mother church, founded in 1866. The present foundation has had five church buildings erected on it. The most recent dedication was in 1981, and the small congregation of singing, shouting Baptists continues strong in spirit.

A third Baptist church began meeting up on the hill on the north side of North Webster in February of 1924. The Reverend S. T. Tyler organized the new church with the help of Baptist ministers from Kirkwood, Webster Groves, and Clayton. They named the new church the Nazarene Baptist Church. The congregation built a small stucco church building on Willis Avenue. Since its beginning the Nazarene Baptist Church has always had an outstanding gospel choir.

Douglass School made great strides in the 1920s also. The Douglass PTA began meeting in 1920. Professor Thomas A. Moore organized night school classes in reading, writing, and sewing.

In 1925 Professor Moore retired, and Herbert S. Davis became the principal of Douglass School. Sumner High School in St. Louis was crowded, and the tuition expense had become too great for the Webster Groves School Board, so the board decided it would be more economical to create a "High School Department" at Douglass. Three rooms and three teachers were added so that in the fall of 1925, Douglass had classes through ninth grade. Adding another grade each year, Davis had established a complete high-school curriculum by the fall of 1928.

Herbert Davis was an excellent choice to oversee the creation of Douglass High School. He was smart and dynamic and had earned a master's degree from the University of Illinois. He sent requests for faculty to many large universities, and he hired fine teachers. His wife, Lorraine, who taught English and Latin, had a master's degree from the University of Illinois. Howell B. Goins came to Douglass to teach social studies in 1926. He had graduated from George R. Smith University in Sedalia, where Scott Joplin had gone to school. Davis hired other teachers, including Ruth Dixon, who came from the University of Nebraska to teach English literature and dramatics; John W. Palmer, who came from Lincoln University to teach math; P. K. Boulding, who came from Geneva College in Pennsylvania to teach history and social studies; Alice Armstrong, who came from the University of Kansas to teach art; and Conrad Thomas, who came from the University of Kansas to teach science, biology, physics, and chemistry.

After his first year of teaching, Thomas spent the entire summer and part of the next year creating the science department in the basement of Douglass. He put in lab tables and chemistry equipment, built floor-to-ceiling shelves along one wall, filling them with treasures from nature and jars of specimens, and put a huge sea aquarium and cages of snakes and mice along another wall. Eventually the science department expanded to include a lecture room.

Nothing seemed impossible to Davis, even though he had to run Douglass with old used books from the white schools. He created a school lunchroom run by the domestic science teacher and her students. The Douglass Drama Class placed first and third in the state competition for 1927. Davis began summer school at Douglass in 1928. The PTA purchased a movie projector for the school so that movies could be shown there on Friday nights. The first high-school graduation from Douglass took place in May 1929. The graduates in that first class were Mattie Gill, Louis Harden, David Hawkins, Thelma Meeks, Mayda Morgan, Helen Morton, Imelda Thomas, and Robert Thomas.

On several occasions Davis requested the use of the Webster Groves High School facilities. In 1927 he asked if the high school could be used for a dance sponsored by the Douglass PTA. In 1929 he asked to use the gym for athletics during the evening. And in May of 1929 he inquired whether the first Douglass high-school graduation ceremony could be held in the auditorium. He was told, "The law will not permit of such use." In the late summer of 1929 he left Douglass and began commuting into St. Louis to teach social studies at the new Vashon High School.

During Herbert Davis's years at Douglass, the PTA became active. The association raised funds for equipment, including band instruments, uniforms, and gym suits, and sponsored parties and dances for the students. Ethel (Stone) Frost was an enthusiastic member of the PTA. She was as eager to improve the quality of education as her father, Frank Stone, had been. She believed that to achieve quality education, it was important for parents and teachers to work together, and for local PTAs to organize statewide to share ideas and support. Because her husband worked for the railroad, Ethel was able to travel free across the state, helping schools organize PTAs and encouraging state and national membership. In 1927 she helped to organize the Missouri Congress of Colored Parents and Teachers, which became the Missouri Branch of the National Congress of Colored Parents and Teachers in 1928. Ethel Frost was elected branch president.

North Webster was producing leaders, and it was attracting leaders and professionals. In 1927 Joseph E. Mitchell moved to Webster Groves. He and his wife had come from Alabama to visit the 1904 World's Fair and had decided to stay in St. Louis. In 1912 Mitchell had founded the *St. Louis Argus,* which became the city's largest Negro weekly newspaper. He was active in politics, a staunch Republican, loyal to the party of Abraham Lincoln, until 1933, when he and many blacks switched their support to Franklin D. Roosevelt and the Democratic Party. Through the *Argus* and his involvement in politics, Mitchell did much to promote the progress of blacks in St. Louis. He was also a strong supporter of the YMCA.

Mitchell built a large, three-story brick house on North Elm Avenue, on a hill that had been an orchard. The house was designed by black architect H. A. Bostic of Tuskegee Institute, and it was built by men from North Webster. Augustus Ewing earned enough money to put himself through college by working on the construction. When the house was finished, it was the grandest home in North Webster. The living room and library were the site of many YMCA and Douglass PTA meetings. The basement had a large kitchen opening onto the back lawn, and it fed many large gatherings. The property had a stable and horses, gardens, a grape arbor, an orchard, and a tennis court. Mitchell invited the young people of North Webster to use his tennis court, and he purchased baseball and other recreational equipment for them to use on his estate.

Among the other professionals who moved to North Webster in the 1920s were Dr. A. Leroy Reynolds and Dr. Eric C. Donnelly. Both physicians graduated from Meharry Medical College in Nashville, Tennessee, one of only two medical schools for blacks in the United States (the other being Howard University in Washington, D.C.). The two doctors lived on Shady Avenue, next door to each other. Dr. Reynolds had his office in the back of his house on the basement level. Dr. Donnelly had his office on the first floor of his house, and his family lived upstairs. Both doctors made house calls. Dr. Reynolds sometimes stayed all night, drinking coffee with a family whose child was sick. Tall, willowy Dr. Donnelly loped off on foot over the hills of North Webster to deliver babies at home. Some children thought he brought the babies in the black satchel that he always carried when he made house calls. When Dr. Reynolds died in the late 1940s, Dr. Thomas Rusan of Richmond Heights took over his practice. Dr. Frazier Alexander opened a doctor's office at the corner of Ravine and Kirkham at that time.

Another professional, Elvis Summytt, moved to North Webster in the mid-1920s. A graduate of Creighton University in Nebraska, he worked for the state as a food-and-drug inspector. When a new administration let him go in 1929, he purchased the Rogers Ice Cream Parlor on North Elm and turned it into the first and only drugstore in North Webster. Besides filling prescriptions, Summytt's Drug Store also sold sandwiches at lunch and ice cream after school. Summytt's had a dance hall in the back, which became the first gymnasium for Douglass School. It was a good place to practice basketball, but too small for a real game. The Douglass team played official basketball games—against Sumner, St. Charles, and Lovejoy and Lincoln from Illinois—at the Pine Street YMCA in St. Louis. The drugstore also had an outdoor garden with tables and benches, and on summer evenings the Summytts hired a band. In the 1930s Dr. J. L. Grigsby, a dentist, and Dr. E. A. South, a surgeon, had offices at Summytt's Drug Store. The Summytts had no children of their own, but they adopted five children and put them through school. Lee Etta Summytt was active in local women's clubs, including the League of Women Voters.

Dixon's Grocery Store at the end of North Elm on Waymire was the final addition to North Webster in the late 1920s. William Dixon came from Aberdeen, Mississippi. His son, J. C. Dixon, had left Aberdeen in a hurry to avoid a lynching; he moved first to St. Louis and then to North Webster, where he started his own hauling business. In 1927 Will Dixon moved to North Webster to be near his son, and opened a little grocery store. By the 1930s Dixon had added a DX filling station in front and a tavern in the back, and he sold ice cream from a side window. Dixon's delivered groceries, and Will's grandson, Hutcher, drove the delivery truck. When Will died of a heart attack in 1944, J. C. took over the business until it closed in 1969.

Much had changed in North Webster in the twenties, and in May 1929, the city of Webster Groves changed the name of Shady Avenue to Kirkham Avenue.

Another change occurred in the early 1930s: the death of an old soldier. In 1932 Andrew Evans was the last surviving soldier of the Civil War in Webster Groves. He occupied the position of honor in the Memorial Day Parade. People applauded as he rode past in an open car decorated with flags and flowers. He was escorted to the soldiers' monument at Lockwood and Big Bend, where he raised a huge United States flag above the monument as bugles played. Evans had been a slave in Franklin County, Missouri. His master freed him after Lincoln's Emancipation Proclamation in 1863, when he was eighteen years old. He walked to St. Louis to enlist in the Union Army, but he was too young, so he went to Illinois and enlisted as a substitute. Evans joined Company E of the Seventeenth United States Colored Infantry, but like many black soldiers he was disappointed at not being allowed to fight. After the war he returned to Franklin County to work for his former master for wages. Evans accumulated farm land of his own, married, and had twelve children. His wife died in 1893, and in 1903 he married again and moved to Webster Groves. When Evans was seventy years old, he learned to read so that he could read the Bible, the newspaper, and letters from his children. When he died in November of 1932, Evans owned two houses and a 1928 Ford. He was one of the last residents of North Webster who had actually been a slave.

There was another old soldier in North Webster, a veteran of the Spanish-American War. Colonel John G. Buford lived at the northern boundary of North Webster, in a house that overhung Deer Creek. He subsisted on his small pension, raising squabs, which he sold to wealthy families of Webster Groves. He flew the American flag from a tall flagpole, and on every national holiday he put on his old uniform and marched down Wellington and up Kirkham with his sword at his side. History teachers invited him to Douglass to tell of his adventures in the Battle of San Juan Hill with Teddy Roosevelt and the Rough Riders. Buford had been in the vanguard of U.S. soldiers assembled at the base of Kettle Hill and San Juan Hill, overlooking Santiago, Cuba, when Roosevelt became impatient and spurred his horse up Kettle Hill. The bugle had not yet sounded the attack, so none of Roosevelt's Rough Riders followed him. The black Ninth and Tenth regiments followed Roosevelt's charge and captured Kettle Hill, clearing the way for the Rough Riders to take San Juan Hill. Few history books tell the story of the Rough Riders and San Juan Hill that way, how two black regiments saved Roosevelt's life. But the students at Douglass knew of the bravery of the Ninth and Tenth regiments and continued to be awed by the proud old soldier who paraded in his uniform down Wellington and up Kirkham, well into the 1940s.

The 1930s brought dramatic changes to Douglass School. After Herbert Davis left in 1929, Howell B. Goins became the principal. Goins was born in Louisiana, Missouri, in 1899, the son of a physician. After graduating from George R. Smith University, he served as the principal of Dunbar School in Elsberry, Missouri, for five years. He taught social studies at Douglass for three years, then took over the administration of Douglass: the elementary, junior high, and high school. Goins continued what Davis had begun. But whereas Davis seemed frustrated by the used books and the discriminatory practices of the school board, Goins seemed to be challenged to prove that excellence is the antidote for discrimination.

In 1931 Goins convinced the Webster Groves School Board to add the gymnasium, the office, and the library to Douglass. Because blacks were allowed to use the Webster Groves Public Library only one afternoon a week, Goins and the residents of North Webster began their own library at Douglass, available to the whole community and open all year. Cyrus B. Taylor came from Hampton Institute to teach industrial arts and to coach a winning basketball team in the new gym.

Goins was strict with his students and his teachers. He expected teachers to set an example for the students. He did not allow women to teach if they got married, and he encouraged teachers who lived in the city to rent a room in North Webster, usually at the big Mitchell house.

In 1932 Douglass High School was accredited by the North Central Association. In 1937 the city and school district of Berkeley, in north St. Louis County, changed their boundaries to exclude Kinloch, a small middle-class black community, thereby creating a tiny all-black school district. In 1939 the school district of Kinloch built the second public high school for blacks in St. Louis County. But the Kinloch School District had the lowest tax base of any school district in the state, and its high school was never accredited by the North Central Association. Douglass remained the only accredited high school for blacks in St. Louis County until all schools were integrated after 1954.

Students came from all over to attend Douglass. They came from communities in St. Louis County, such as Kirkwood, Kinloch, Berkeley, Richmond Heights, Brentwood, Clayton, Ladue, Ferguson, Florissant, Manchester, Glencoe, and Valley Park; and from communities outside the county, such as Pacific and Washington, Missouri, over forty miles away. The school districts paid tuition, and there was no bussing. Some students took the train at six in the morning, and some rode the streetcar.

Goins began offering night school in the spring of 1933. It was so popular that in the fall he expanded it to four nights a week under the Federal Emergency Fund for Education. He put unemployed teachers to work, and the school glowed with activities for a large part of the community every evening. In 1934 he added the cafeteria, the kindergarten, an addition to the shop, new equipment for the home economics department, and a larger library with a loan from the Federal Emergency Administration of Public Works. During the Depression, Goins and the school board took advantage of as many of Franklin Roosevelt's programs as they could. Goins helped students find scholarships for college and part-time work through the National Youth Administration. He stressed academics, discipline, and homework. Each classroom had only nine or ten students, so teachers were able to give students as much individual attention as they would get in a private school.

Boys who thought of goofing off, or even just daydreaming, had only to look out the school window on a gray winter day to be reminded of how important their education was. Outside in the bitter cold, men of the area who had not finished school did hard labor for the gas company. They wore tattered coats, and their hands and feet were bound up in rags because they had no gloves or shoes. The white foreman for the gas company sat in his warm truck drinking hot coffee, while the cheap labor he had recruited that morning struck the frozen ground over and over with pickaxes, digging a trench for new gas lines. The Depression motivated students to do their best, aided by the old women who sat on their front porches all evening and knew everything that went on, including every minor transgression by every neighborhood teenager. "Henry St. James, you came home late last night. Shame on you."

Down at the north end of town, three bridges spanned the creeks. An old wooden bridge crossed Shady Creek at Wellington Avenue, a larger cement bridge crossed Deer Creek where Shady Avenue became North and South Road, and an iron trestle for the Kirkwood-Ferguson streetcar crossed Deer Creek in front of Jim's Market. A group of men perched like crows on the railing of the old wooden Wellington Avenue bridge. All day long, in any weather, they sat in the shade of the giant sycamore trees, and even when the trees were bare, talking about life and waiting for work.

The creeks meant a lot to North Webster. All along Deer Creek, east and west of the place where Shady Creek emptied into it, the fishing was good. Many in the community gathered along Deer Creek in the evening and on weekends to catch their dinner and socialize. Carl Walker was always among them, preaching the latest ideas from Marcus Garvey.

But sometimes the creeks were cruel. In the 1920s the spring-fed water gave children typhoid. The creeks were always flooding; every spring the families along the banks of Shady Creek had to flee with all their possessions to higher ground. Sometimes the Red Cross rescued them from their houses in rowboats. During the 1930s the WPA rerouted Shady Creek through large culverts to try to control the flooding.

For years a quarry operated along Deer Creek at the intersection of Kirkham and Marshall avenues. Men from the quarry knocked on the doors of the houses along Kirkham to warn residents when they were going to blast. Government officials, believing that blasting contributed to the flooding, finally closed the quarry.

One of the boys of North Webster recognized an opportunity to help support his family with the loose rock that the quarry left behind in the creek. Benny Gordon moved to Webster Groves with his mother and younger brother during the depths of the Depression, when he was ten years old. His mother married the Reverend John J. Blackburn, an interim minister at the First Baptist Church, the very day they arrived. But the Reverend Blackburn was often away from home, sometimes preaching at distant churches and sometimes finding employment with the WPA or the CCC. Annie Blackburn raised her two sons and a niece and nephew by herself on her small salary as a domestic. She and the four children lived in a three-room shack next to Shady Creek. They could see daylight through the roof, and when it rained they put buckets on the beds to keep the blankets dry. In winter they stuffed the chinks in the walls with rags or newspapers, and Benny carried water for the family from the free hydrant which the city had installed in the St. James pasture. Every spring when the creek flooded, Annie Blackburn took her children to stay with friends who lived on higher ground.

Benny supplemented his mother's small income by selling the limestone rock from the creek for landscaping. The Howe brothers took orders for him over the telephone at their grocery store. Benny loaded the rock into Clyde Harris's truck, and he and Harris delivered it. Benny charged five dollars a ton, and he guessed at the weight.

When Benny Gordon graduated from high school, his mother gave him the only present she could afford, her beautiful handkerchief. Her small gift reminded Benny of a story from the New Testament about a poor widow who contributed two mites to the church, causing Jesus to observe to his disciples, "This poor widow hath cast more into the treasury than all they who have cast into the treasury, for they cast in from their abundance, but she from her want cast in all that she had." Benny carried his mother's handkerchief, her widow's mite, with him for good luck when he went away to college and all through World War II.

William Dew was another enterprising youth in North Webster during the Depression. He never finished high school, but he was a mechanical genius. He built a steam engine out of tin cans and put automobiles together in his driveway on Cornell. His ability with engines became legendary, and the biggest automobile dealers in St. Louis came to North Webster to find him when they had cars that would not run. On one occasion the city of Webster Groves purchased a new La France fire engine that would not start. Even the salesman and mechanic from La France were unable to get it started. At last someone said, "Let's try William Dew." Dew came to the fire station and had the engine running in no time. William Dew died of a severe infection when he was still in his twenties.

Policy men were the true entrepreneurs of the 1930s. They sold chances on the numbers games for twenty-five cents apiece. Every afternoon they rode the streetcar to the Booker T. Washington Hotel at Jefferson and Pine in St. Louis, where they turned in large sums of money and waited to hear the winning numbers. The odds were tremendous, one hundred to one, or better. But it was unwise to bet more than a dollar, because if a large bet won, the policy men claimed that it had broken the bank and refused to pay. It was also popular to bet on the weather, buying chances on a specific temperature at a specific hour. Policy men brought excitement to North Webster during the Depression.

For entertainment, folks rode the streetcar in to the nightclubs and music halls in Mill Creek Valley, where Scott Joplin and Tom Turpin played ragtime and W. C. Handy introduced the blues. They went to the Booker T. Washington Theater at 23rd and Walnut to see performers such as Josephine Baker, Bessie Smith, and Eubie Blake in the 1920s. In the late 1930s, Jordan Chambers opened the Riviera Nightclub on Delmar, offering performances by Cab Calloway, Lionel Hampton, Count Basie, Dinah Washington, Sarah Vaughn, Ella Fitzgerald, and Jimmie Lunceford. At the Castle Ballroom, people danced to live music by Cab Calloway, Louis Jordan, and Andy Kirk. Blacks rode the streetcars or their bicycles to the movies at the Star Theater on Jefferson at Walnut, the Strand at 21st and Market, the Douglass Theater on Finney, the Comet at Sarah and Finney, the Criterion on Franklin, the Amethyst Theater in the Poro Building on Pendleton, and the Roosevelt Theater on Leffingwell. They enjoyed the best hamburgers at Billie Burke's in the Ville, and the best fried chicken at the Deluxe on Jefferson in Mill Creek Valley. People from North Webster went to the West End Waiters Club on Vandeventer to hear such local talent as Chick Finney, Dewey Jackson, Harry Wynn, Jimmy Forest, the Pillar Brothers, and Ruth Brown.

Three smaller nightclubs flourished in the unincorporated area of North Webster. The Rainbow, at Waymire and Bell, was the fanciest nightclub, sitting discreetly off the road so that no one could see who was inside. The large hall had a dance floor in the center, surrounded by tables with linen tablecloths, and a jukebox played music, except on the nights when a live band performed. A bar on one side of the room served beer and soda all week. At midnight on Saturday that bar closed, and the bar on the other side of the room sold 3.2 percent beer all day Sunday. Customers wanting whiskey brought their own. Arthur

Stewart owned the Rainbow. Stewart, who was the chauffeur for the Warren family in Webster Groves for more than thirty years, was a local political leader, a staunch Republican.

Piggy's was the only dive in North Webster. The dark little storefront with a jukebox and tables served beer and liquor from a long bar. The pool hall next door had gambling in the back. When there was trouble at Piggy's, the police never came, because they were not responsible for the unincorporated area of St. Louis County. Randolph "Piggy" North operated Piggy's. William Bobbit built and owned the building. Bobbit started out as a contractor who demolished old buildings and sold the used materials. He was an enterprising businessman and owned a large lumberyard in East St. Louis.

The Vendome was the oldest nightclub and the most popular. The low, flat, rambling place sat on short stilts at the end of Truesdale Avenue, down in the "Bottoms" by Deer Creek. One year an early spring flood swept the Vendome off its stilt foundation and would have washed it away, but luckily the building caught in the big sycamore trees along the bank of the creek.

Joe Turner owned the Vendome. He named it for the Place Vendome, a fashionable square in Paris in front of the Ritz Hotel. His brother, Henry, had served in France during World War I. Like other black soldiers, Henry often told of the lack of discrimination in Paris after World War I and of the romantic atmosphere of the Place Vendome.

The Vendome sold hot dogs, beer, and soda. Short, fat "Boobie" Williams, sporting an old black derby and garters on his sleeves, sat at the upright piano playing ragtime, loud and fast. There was a pool table and gambling in the back room.

Joe Turner also owned the large playing field that spread out in front of the Vendome. Some folks called it the Bottoms, but it was so lush and beautiful that others with a highbrow sense of humor called it Riverside Park. When Turner fenced the playing field in order to charge admission, he named it Riverside Stadium. Actually, there were no bleachers, and patrons sat in the grass.

Three outstanding teams played at Riverside Stadium. Dave Wilkins coached the Webster Reds football team, and Joe Turner himself, smoking a fat cigar, coached the Webster Reds baseball team. People came from all over to watch the outstanding baseball team play, including white folks from Webster Groves, among them Andy McDonald, the chief of police, and Harry Caray, the future sports announcer. The Webster Reds played against both black and white baseball teams. They played the great Powell Grocery team from Meacham Park in Kirkwood and teams from Desoto, Festus, and Herculaneum, Missouri; East St. Louis and Sparta, Illinois; and Evansville, Indiana. They traveled to out-of-town games in an open truck, but they played like pros. The team dissolved during World War II, but in the early 1950s some Douglass High School students actually became professionals. Alphonse Smith played for the Cleveland Indians and hit a home run in the 1954 World Series. He went on to play for the Baltimore Orioles and the Chicago White Sox. Charles and Clarence Hall played for the Pittsburgh Pirates in the minor league.

The Howe brothers, owners of the grocery store on Kirkham, started the third team that played at Riverside Stadium, the Blue Valley Giants, a baseball team for boys between the ages of ten and fourteen. The Howe brothers got the Blue Valley Creamery to sponsor the boys for their Blue Valley League. The Blue Valley Giants, the only black team in the league, played against teams from Brentwood, Ladue, University City, and South St. Louis, and they usually won.

On several occasions in the spring, gypsies camped at Riverside Park in the Bottoms. They came in Pierce Arrows and Dusenbergs, pitching fancy striped tents by the creek, and covering the ground inside the tents with Oriental rugs. Residents of North Webster and Webster Groves feared that the gypsies would rob their houses and kidnap their children. The police did nothing because the Bottoms was an unincorporated area. But those residents who were not afraid went down to watch the gypsies make willow furniture during the day, and sing and dance with castanets and accordions around the campfire at night. They sold the willow furniture door to door in North Webster. In the spring of 1935, the queen of the gypsies was married in a lavish ceremony in the Bottoms. Each year, in less than a week, the gypsies were gone as suddenly as they had come.

White politicians were almost as entertaining as the gypsies during the Depression. In the summer each one gave a barbecue in Preble Salmon's side yard or somebody's backyard, or in the empty lot in front of the Rainbow. While residents of North Webster stood around or sat on benches, eating hot dogs and drinking beer and soda, the candidate gave a speech about how much better things would be if people voted for him. Near election time, the candidates went door to door handing out calling cards with their names and faces on them. But when the election was over, nothing changed in North Webster. The streets did not get paved, and sewers were not installed. The politicians helped a few people get St. Louis County government jobs in the coroner's office, in the deputy sheriff's office, and with the recorder of deeds. In the meantime, improvements had to come from the community itself.

In 1939 a group of concerned citizens decided that something had to be done about the tragic fires which destroyed three or four homes every year. The fires usually started from dangerous coal oil stoves, and because neighboring fire departments would not answer calls from the unincorporated area, neighbors had to watch helplessly as the houses burned to the ground. In 1939 John C. Dixon, Walter Pierpont Ewing, Roscoe James, Herbert Witt, Clyde Harris, Lewis Bryant, Rubin Talbert, Emma Ewing, and Ardelia Harris Montgomery met at Dixon's store and organized the North Webster Volunteer Firefighters Association. They bought a secondhand fire truck and operated out of Dixon's garage for over a year, until they raised enough money to build the North Webster Firehouse. The money came from the annual sale of Volunteer Firefighters Association tags, which hung prominently on each house in North Webster, and from the proceeds of the North Webster Carnival.

The North Webster Carnival brought the entire community together each summer for almost thirty years. It was held in late June or early July in the large vacant lot on top of the hill at Lithia and Bell. Friday night, all day Saturday, and on Sunday after church, the music of the merry-go-round and the lights of the Ferris wheel attracted children and the young-at-heart from all around. Carnival people from High Hill, Missouri, provided rides, games, and cotton candy. The firefighters sold barbecue, spaghetti, and hot dogs, and the ladies of the Firefighters Association sold homemade potato salad, coleslaw, and baked goods.

The carnival and the fire tags did not make enough money to keep the firehouse and the pumper operating all year, so Walter Pierpont Ewing, who was one of the builders of the firehouse, ran a concession there selling barbecue, hot dogs, and soda, and renting the building for dances. From the beginning, the twenty or so volunteer firemen succeeded in putting out all fires.

The community established another successful institution for itself, the North Webster Credit Union. Before 1947, no bank in Webster Groves would give a black person a small loan. That year Herbert Davis, the former principal, who was then teaching at Vashon, suggested that North Webster organize a credit union. Mosby Collins, the barber, invested the first one thousand dollars. Members purchased shares in the North Webster Credit Union for five dollars a share. The credit union charged 4 percent interest and rarely granted loans larger than fifty dollars. Roscoe James served as president and loan officer of the association for many years. The office remained in his basement, under various loan officers, until the North Webster Credit Union merged with the West Community Credit Union in Brentwood in 1978.

The residents of North Webster provided everything they needed for themselves. There were great places for young people to go after school, including Johnson's Restaurant on North Elm, with a dance hall in the back where young people jitterbugged around the jukebox. When Hubbard's Confectionery at Holland and Ravine became Granbery's Brown Bobby Shop, everyone continued to stop there after school for Brown Bobby donuts. Those who commuted to Douglass from other parts of St. Louis County stopped at the Shady Nook, on Kirkham at Ravine, before they took the streetcar home. DeWitt Davis owned the Shady Nook and made the juiciest hamburgers for miles around.

In 1944 the PTA, led by Walter Rusan, raised nine thousand dollars to build a YMCA at Holland and Ravine, in order to provide more structure for young people. The one-story colonial building hosted Hi-Y meetings and weekend movies. Membership in the Y provided access to the swimming pool and basketball court at the Pine Street YMCA and the Phyllis Wheatley YWCA in St. Louis. Joseph E. Mitchell, the editor of the *St. Louis Argus,* had been eager for North Webster to have its own YMCA. An active supporter of the Pine Street YMCA, he had sponsored Y activities for young people at his home in Webster Groves. In 1944 he contributed generously to the new North Webster YMCA.

Mitchell did other things for black youth. He sponsored the Worthy Boys' Dinner at the Pine Street Y for five hundred underprivileged boys each year and served on the board of directors of the Annie Malone Children's Home. Governor Phil Donnelly appointed Mitchell to the Missouri State Board of Education, and Governor Forrest Smith continued his appointment to that board. His greatest honor came in 1944, when the Democratic Party made him a presidential elector. Mitchell visited President Franklin D. Roosevelt at the White House, and in later years he was a close friend of President Harry Truman.

Perhaps it was too early for a black man to be held in such high esteem and to own such a fancy home in a prosperous suburb, for in December 1944, the Webster Groves School Board began proceedings to condemn J. E. Mitchell's property, under the right of eminent domain, in order to build a new elementary school.

For some time the Douglass PTA had been asking for a new school. Three of the elementary classes were meeting in temporary portable structures on the playground behind Douglass. The rest of the 230 elementary children and the 330 junior high and high-school students and twenty-six teachers attended classes in the old building which had begun as two rooms in 1892. In April 1944, a committee of the Douglass PTA met with the school board to impress upon them the disadvantages of having elementary children in the same building as high-school students. Discipline was difficult. Young children were using the same facilities as teenagers.

The school board agreed that the community needed a new elementary school, and the residents of Webster Groves passed a bond issue in December 1944 to finance the construction of Douglass Elementary School and a new gymnasium at the white high school. The school board considered building on the eight empty acres which it owned north of Douglass, but it then decided to acquire all the land in the same block as the old Douglass School, including the Mitchell mansion. Mitchell did not want to leave his home, but he finally signed a contract agreeing to vacate in May 1945. The board threatened to condemn his property if he was not out by January 15, 1945. The families of North Webster were afraid to speak out on Mitchell's behalf for fear of losing the badly needed new school. Mitchell moved into the city in March 1945, and the new Douglass Elementary School opened in the fall of 1947. Now North Webster had two schools: the modern, brick Douglass Elementary School on North Elm Avenue, and the old frame-and-stucco Douglass High School behind it on Holland Avenue. Howell B. Goins, whose office was in the new Douglass Elementary School, was the principal of both.

Douglass School was an inspiration for its students. The faculty, as members of a minority and residents of a closely knit community, looked upon the students as their own children, as their legacy. To get ahead in a segregated society, these children had to excel. Douglass School taught them to excel, through classwork and extracurricular activities.

The teachers offered an impressive selection of extracurricular activities. Imelda Wyatt, the kindergarten teacher, taught ballet and tap dancing on Saturdays. A seventh- and eighth-grade hobby club was popular with the boys, and Junior Red Cross, the dramatics club, and the camera club occupied other teens. In the early thirties, Alice Armstrong took her art classes on field trips to the City Art Museum. Art students and ceramics students won awards under instructor Wilbert Berry in the forties and fifties. The Etiquette Club and Entre Nous taught manners, poise, and the art of entertaining. Hortense Pharries sponsored the Home Economics Club and the New Homemakers of America. Louvan Gearin, the librarian, organized the Teenage Book Club.

Scouting began at Douglass in the early 1930s. Conrad Thomas, the science teacher, led the Boy Scout troop. When he took the boys camping at Lion's Den or Lone Dell, the two wilderness camps for blacks in the St. Louis Boy Scout Council, he continued their science education. The Girl Scouts met at the homes of several leaders. Gladys Anderson and Harriet Ashcraft, the third- and fourth-grade teachers, led the Brownie troops, and Mrs. Conrad Thomas took groups of Girl Scouts, with their picnic lunches, on the streetcar named "The Dinky" into the St. Louis Girl Scout Council Day Camp in Forest Park.

A huge choir, a smaller choral group, an orchestra, and a band performed at Douglass. Naomi White directed them until 1935, and Earl Eulingburgh from 1935 to 1940. In 1940 Principal Goins went down to Cairo, Illinois, to recruit Walter Lathen to direct the music department. Lathen created a wonderful sixty-piece band, which received the highest honors at the state music festivals and integrated the Suburban Music Educators' Association. Students stayed after school and came at night to rehearse. The PTA chartered buses for the band to travel to music festivals, and they brought other bands to Douglass to give concerts. Kenneth Billups, who later became the choral director of the St. Louis Symphony, taught vocal music at Douglass from 1943 to 1949.

Douglass School held three big dances each year: a homecoming dance during the football season, a dance at which Miss Douglass was crowned during the basketball season, and the senior prom. Jeanette Gleason was crowned the first Miss Douglass in 1934. She and her twin brother, James, were outstanding students and leaders at the school. They both went on to Lincoln University, but Jeanette became ill and died before she graduated. Her mother, Mildred Lipscomb, established the Jeanette Gleason Scholarship, which the PTA awarded to a deserving student each year.

Maurice Grant taught social studies and business and sponsored the Newspaper Club, which published the school paper, the *Hi Echo*. Melzetta Frost started the school paper, pushing students to meet impossible deadlines, and also taught typing and business education. She began teaching in 1936 with six typewriters in a small room behind the office. She decided to make the business education department equivalent to a fine secretarial school, and she was soon teaching shorthand, business English, bookkeeping, and how to operate a mimeograph machine. Her classes did all the mimeograph work for Douglass School and for other community organizations. By the 1950s she had thirty-three typewriters and was finding her students good secretarial jobs when they graduated.

Thurston Graham advised the Honors Society. He taught civics, French, and Spanish and made arrangements for students in his Spanish classes to correspond with families in South America. One of his students became an interpreter, and another worked for the State Department.

P. K. Boulding taught history and social studies. After school he sponsored the Human Relations Club, at which students discussed community problems with members of local churches, the city government, and the school board. Dorothy Boulding taught physical education, health, and English and sponsored the Girls' Athletic Association and the Douglass cheerleaders. Wilbert Berry, the art instructor, advised the student government, the Douglass majorettes, and the flag twirlers. William Bell, the physical education instructor, sponsored the Leaders' Club and coached the outstanding football, basketball, and track teams. Bell was popular with the students because he was a fabulous dancer and promoted school talent shows and parties.

The football and basketball games attracted Douglass students, families, and alumni from all over St. Louis County. In North Webster, the entire community went to the games. Local stores closed. Before a football game, the stream of people was like a parade up Holland Avenue and down the trail through the St. James pasture to the football field in the Bottoms. The cheerleaders, the majorettes, the flag twirlers, the band, and the football team poured out of Douglass School down the trail onto the field, sending a thrill through the crowd. In 1945 the Douglass football team became the Missouri state champions and the Illinois-Missouri League champions. Kenneth Billups had written "Hail to Douglass," the school song, in 1943. "Hail to Douglass, dear old school," rang out over the hills. "Purple and gold, fight on."

Then the war began to take away the boys of Douglass. Donald Monroe was the first to die. Monroe was one of several orphans adopted and raised during the Depression by Nannie Stewart, the truant officer. He joined the navy before the United States entered the war and was killed at Pearl Harbor. American Legion Post #375 in North Webster was named in his honor.

When war was declared in December 1941, the Selective Service expanded its age limits and raised the quota of men required from each local draft board. By 1944 all the eligible men from Webster Groves had gone to war, and the Selective Service office on North Gore was drafting boys as soon as they turned eighteen. Some boys from Douglass School, including Carl Hall, his brother, Wardie Hall, and Arthur Hinch, were taken before they could graduate. Arthur Hinch had enough credits and was able to come home on furlough to graduate with his class. Wardie Hall finished his senior year and graduated after the war ended.

The armed services were still segregated during World War II. Blacks trained, lived, and fought in separate units from whites. Most black units were enlisted as labor units to dig trenches, drive trucks, and cook. Therefore, approximately 10 percent of America's armed forces were not allowed to fight until the Allies began suffering a severe manpower shortage as they battled across France, after the invasion of Normandy, in 1944. At that time the army began retraining volunteers from black units for the infantry.

Many black soldiers volunteered for service in the Third Army under General George S. Patton. "Old Blood and Guts" Patton had a reputation for expecting the same hard work from all his men no matter what their color, and for never asking his men to do anything that he would not do himself. Walter Ambrose of North Webster served in Third Army Headquarters with General Patton, reporting troop strength and fuel and supply strengths to Patton at the 8:00 A.M. morning report every day. When Sergeant Major Ambrose hand-delivered orders from General Dwight D. Eisenhower to General Patton stating that no Negro soldiers were to receive furloughs for Paris, Patton was furious and sent back a memo which said, "I was not aware the Third Army had Negro soldiers, only American soldiers."

Harry Rogers of North Webster was an MP who directed traffic for supply convoys in Italy, interweaving the supply trucks at a constant speed with the hordes of refugees moving through the intersections of each little town.

Perhaps the greatest contribution made by black soldiers to the war in Europe was the supply convoy across France known as the Red Ball Express. After landing on the coast of western France in the summer of 1944, the Allies could not move food, fuel, and ammunition fast enough to keep up with their armies moving east toward Germany, because bridges and rail lines had been destroyed. Black truck drivers of the Motor Transport Brigade, inspired by years of experience with high-priority Red Ball freight trains, commandeered two parallel roads across northern France to be used as one-way highways by the remarkable Red Ball Express. All other traffic was prohibited from the designated routes, and the enthusiastic drivers sped east along the northern road and back along the southern road at a constant speed, always sixty yards apart. Every truck had a large red ball painted on each side of the radiator hood to identify it as part of the special convoy. Drivers took turns driving day and night, through all kinds of danger, their headlights defying the blackout, stopping only for exactly ten minutes before every second hour. Without the Red Ball Express, Generals Patton and Montgomery could not have kept up their rapid advances and would not have reached Germany before the deadly winter snow.

The valiant Tuskegee Airmen also served in the European Theater of the war. James Gleason of North Webster received a Bronze Star as a Tuskegee Airman. In July 1941, the War Department established the Ninety-ninth Pursuit Squadron of Tuskegee Institute, in Tuskegee, Alabama, as a training experiment. It was a sharp break with military tradition, which held that blacks were not suited for fighting, flying fighter planes, or command. After successful training, the Tuskegee Airmen were not given a combat mission until 1943, when they were sent to North Africa, Sicily, and finally the Anzio Beachhead in Italy. At first, officers of the Army Air Corps criticized the Tuskegee Experiment, but after the victory at Anzio Beachhead, the Tuskegee Airmen received much acclaim. During the rest of the war, providing air support in the Balkans, Romania, Czechoslovakia, Austria, France, and Germany, the Tuskegee Airmen flew thousands of missions, destroying many enemy planes, and never losing a plane of their own.

These brave soldiers returning home after the war, with the benefits of the GI Bill and the optimism created when President Truman integrated the armed forces in 1948, expected to find less discrimination, good jobs, and nice houses in the old neighborhood. But the majority of the jobs available to them were at restaurants, candy factories, the Liggett and Meyers Tobacco Company, Scullin Steel, the postal service, and the Pullman Company, or as elevator operators or custodians. Their wives could not try on dresses at Famous-Barr, Stix, Baer and Fuller, or Scruggs, Vandervoort and Barney. And no black person could eat at a white restaurant or lunch counter or go to a white theater.

In 1948 George L. Vaughn, a brilliant black lawyer from St. Louis, took the case of *Shelley vs. Kraemer* all the way to the U.S. Supreme Court, to determine whether a restrictive covenant in a deed to property on Labadie Avenue in St. Louis could legally prohibit a Negro from owning that property. The Supreme Court decided that restrictive covenants are contrary to the intent of the Fourteenth Amendment to the Constitution and therefore illegal.

The black neighborhood of North Webster expanded its boundaries several blocks west of Rock Hill Road in the 1950s. But it could go no farther. Although the courts would no longer enforce restrictive covenants, members of the St. Louis Real Estate Exchange still respected color boundaries when showing property to prospective buyers.

When Sergeant Major Benny Gordon returned from his extended

tour of duty in Europe during the war and the Occupation, he ran into another kind of discrimination. He saw an old friend, a Webster Groves city councilman, at Mueller's Drug Store on Gore, and they talked of the changes that had occurred since the war. The councilman was especially proud of the beautiful new municipal swimming pool, dedicated on Memorial Day 1949. Gordon said that it sounded nice and that he would have to go for a swim sometime. The councilman stiffened and replied that the pool was for whites only; maybe someday the city would build a swimming pool for the black community.

The inequality made Gordon simmer as the summer wore on. Neighbors told his mother that he would cause a race riot if he tried to swim in the municipal pool. Finally, on July 2, the hottest day of the summer, Gordon asked Frank Witt if he would drive him to the swimming pool. Erma Calvin and Evalee Wilkerson went with them. The municipal pool attendants would not admit the four young people. As they stood in the parking lot discussing what to do to escape the 102 degree heat, the police, the mayor, and all three city councilmen arrived to warn them not to cause a disturbance.

As the summer faded into fall, Gordon, Witt, Calvin, Wilkerson, and Arthur Green, the director of the North Webster YMCA, discussed hiring George Vaughn, the attorney who had defeated restrictive covenants in St. Louis, to represent them in winning the right for all taxpayers of Webster Groves to swim in the municipal pool. But Vaughn suffered a stroke and died. So the small group asked Theodore McMillian to represent them. McMillian, fresh out of law school, had few clients, and even though the North Webster group had little money, he agreed to take the case.

McMillian contacted the law school at Vanderbilt University in Nashville, Tennessee, to get help with the lawsuit. The *Vanderbilt Law Review* was publishing articles about restrictive covenants and public accommodations such as swimming pools, because Paul Saunders, a young professor of constitutional law, was interested in issues pertaining to segregation. Saunders collected information about any case having to do with segregation anywhere in the country. Eventually he began publishing all such cases in the *Race Relations Law Reporter*. By the 1960s, judges, lawyers, and law schools everywhere subscribed to the newsletter, because it chronicled the titanic changes taking place in America. In the early 1950s, the Vanderbilt Law School was the only place in the country, except for Howard University in Washington, D.C., to which blacks could turn for legal help regarding segregation.

On the day the Webster pool opened for the summer of 1950, Theodore McMillian filed suit in St. Louis County Circuit Court for a temporary injunction to allow Frank Witt, Erma Calvin, and Evalee Wilkerson to use the pool, alleging that they had been denied rights provided under the Fourteenth Amendment to the Constitution of the United States. Judge John Witthaus denied the temporary injunction and rescheduled the trial for September, so that the municipal pool could stay open for whites only during the summer of 1950.

Judge Witthaus heard the case in September and issued his decree on December 18, 1950. He decreed that the action of the defendants (the mayor and three city councilmen) was an exercise of governmental power and as such was a violation of the rights of the plaintiffs and others of the Negro race under the Constitution of the United States and under the Constitution of the State of Missouri.

The Webster Groves City Council decided not to appeal Judge Witthaus's decision. In February 1951 they issued a statement, published in the *Webster News-Times*, refusing to open the swimming pool to anyone during the summer of 1951. The city council claimed that integrating the municipal pool would cause a drop in attendance and a loss of revenue which the city could not afford. Many liberal white residents of Webster Groves were incensed by the policy of the mayor and the three city councilmen. The Reverend James Lichliter of Emmanuel Episcopal Church; the Reverend Ervine Inglis of First Congregational Church; Alfred Lee Booth, music director of Webster Groves Presbyterian Church; Glenn Thomas, editor of the *Webster News-Times;* Robert Turner, an insurance salesman and former minister; Arthur Armstrong, director of the Webster Groves Red Cross; and members of the Webster Groves League of Women Voters and the Goodall PTA worked diligently to open the facility to all Webster residents. Under the leadership of the oldest Webster Groves churches, residents offered to raise enough money to guarantee its operating expenses. But the beautiful pool remained empty during the hot summer of 1951.

In 1952 the city council decided to open the pool three days a week for whites, one day a week for Negroes. Leaders of the black community threatened to fight such an insult in court. The few outspoken leaders of the black community were tired of being treated as second-class citizens. However, most residents of North Webster remained silent on the swimming pool issue. They could not afford to lose their jobs in Webster Groves homes and businesses, and they were afraid of losing their mortgages at the Webster Groves Trust Company. The pool remained closed during the summer of 1952, and Webster Groves residents began calling for a new form of city government.

The city of Webster Groves held an election in 1953, with three big issues on the ballot. The voters elected to open the municipal swimming pool to all residents of Webster Groves; they elected a new mayor and city council; and they elected a Board of Freeholders to write a new city charter. The pool opened on Memorial Day 1953 with police present, and it has operated without a problem ever since.

The newly elected Board of Freeholders included Lorraine Davis, a former teacher at Douglass High School, a member of the League of Women Voters, and a level-headed leader of North Webster. The board wrote a new city charter which was adopted by the citizens of Webster Groves in March of 1954. It gave Webster Groves a city manager form of government and increased the number of councilmen to six, in order to represent a broader spectrum of the community.

It was necessary for a broader spectrum to be represented, for there had been many residents of Webster Groves interested in interracial activities and integration for a long time. In the early 1920s Anne Branch Cushing, the first president of the League of Women Voters of Webster Groves, had organized a special division of the Webster League for black ladies. She wanted the voters of North Webster to be as enlightened as the voters in the rest of Webster Groves.

Students and faculty from Eden Theological Seminary in Webster Groves became interested in interracial activities in the early 1930s. Richard and Reinhold Niebuhr, the great theologians and social reformers, had attended Eden Seminary, and they remained influential, Richard as a faculty member and Reinhold as a member of Eden's board of directors. Eden students played basketball against Douglass students in the thirties, and faculty members from Eden attended meetings of Walter Rusan's Interracial Group at Douglass School in the 1940s and 1950s.

Walter Rusan, a postal worker and the father of two boys, served as president of the Douglass PTA for many years and organized the North Webster YMCA. He devoted much of his life to improving interracial relations in Webster Groves as the president of the Webster Groves Interracial Group. This group, which included many Eden faculty members, organized to obtain sewers for the incorporated part of North Webster in the forties, then began to work on integrating the schools. After Rusan's death in 1970, the Webster Groves School Board dedicated Rusan Field behind Steger Junior High School to his memory, "in recognition of his life-long service to the youth of the area and to the promotion of understanding between races."

In the 1940s, the Reverend W. D. Thompson of the First Baptist Church helped organize the Ministerial Alliance in North Webster to encourage ecumenical community spirit among the black churches. It soon expanded to include the white churches of Webster Groves and became the Webster Groves Ministerial Alliance, focusing on interracial as well as ecumenical activities.

In 1948, representatives of the women's societies of many of the churches in Webster Groves organized the Webster Groves Council of Church Women to foster ecumenical and interracial understanding. The women took turns hosting luncheons at their churches, with speakers on many topics. They became the United Church Women of Webster Groves in 1954 and continued to meet regularly until 1965.

In 1950, the year of the swimming pool lawsuit, Nellie Salmon, a dear old Douglass teacher, died. She surprised the community by leaving her home and her small estate to the Webster Groves Red Cross to establish an interracial day nursery for working mothers. Salmon had originally intended her estate to provide for her blind son, Preble. Preble had been a chauffeur and an electrician before going blind, and he had always been active in Republican politics. But Preble Salmon died in 1949. Nellie Salmon's long-time friend Congressman Tom Curtis helped her write her other dream into her will: an interracial nursery school.

Volunteers from the Webster Groves Interracial Group, the Nursery Committee, the Webster Groves Red Cross, and the First Baptist Church of Webster Groves labored to convert the little house into a school. The Nellie Salmon Day Care Center operated from 1952 until 1957, when it had to close because of financial instability. The funds from the sale of Nellie Salmon's property continued her generous legacy by endowing an annual Nellie Salmon Scholarship for a graduating senior from Webster Groves High School. The scholarship is still awarded each year.

But Nellie Salmon was not the first to integrate education in Missouri, or even in Webster Groves. In 1944 St. Louis University was the first school, at any level, to integrate in Missouri, and the first university to integrate in any of the fifteen original slave states. In 1947 Archbishop Joseph E. Ritter ordered the five high schools of the archdiocese to admit blacks.

The year before, in 1946, Irene Thomas of North Webster had applied for admission to Webster College, an all-white Catholic girls' college in Webster Groves. Irene had started at Stowe Teachers' College in St. Louis, but she wanted to major in music and languages, which were not available at the segregated teachers' college. Webster College admitted Irene with no problem. The Thomas family and the whole community of North Webster were proud of Irene for blazing the trail, but they knew it would be difficult.

Articles in several local papers called Irene a maverick. At the parents' orientation ceremony in the college auditorium, other parents walked out when the Thomases entered. Some of the faculty and students were prejudiced and cruel. It was especially painful when Irene was called into the dean's office and told that her mother could not belong to the Mothers' Club.

But Irene's voice teacher was encouraging, and Irene was stubborn. In 1950 Irene was the first black student to graduate from Webster College. In 1951 the Women's Achievement Association of St. Louis named her mother, Alby Thomas, who could not belong to the Mothers' Club, the Mother of the Year. She certainly deserved the recognition, for Alby and Charles Thomas had struggled to put all nine of their children through college. Their children included five public school teachers, a postal worker, a librarian, the president of a large corporation, and a Head Start teacher.

All of the students at Douglass School learned how to be successful. Douglass students knew all the Negro heroes, such as Crispus Attucks, Frederick Douglass, Harriet Tubman, Sojourner Truth, George Washington Carver, Booker T. Washington, and W. E. B. Du Bois. Those heroes made Douglass students realize how much can be accomplished from a modest beginning with hard work. During National Negro History Week, all the students were involved in special projects, reports, stories, and plays about black history. Famous blacks who were outstanding role models, including Jesse Owens and James Weldon Johnson, came and spoke to the students at assemblies and stayed to sign autographs at lunch. On one occasion the visiting speaker was Carl Sandburg, who was not black but was a good role model. The parents and faculty of Douglass expected the students to go on to college, and that expectation became a self-fulfilling prophecy. The faculty, especially Ruth Dixon, the head of the guidance department, helped students choose colleges and find scholarships. Douglass gave its students a special appreciation for their heritage and their potential that no other school could give them.

Then in 1954 the United States Supreme Court made its momentous decision regarding public education. In the case of *Brown vs. Board of Education of Topeka,* argued by Thurgood Marshall, attorney for the NAACP, the Supreme Court ruled that "separate educational facilities are inherently unequal."

Of the 430 students at Douglass High School, 246 lived outside of Webster Groves, and now they could go to schools in their own communities. While Douglass Elementary School remained open, Douglass High School was closed in 1956. Only seven of the nineteen teachers from Douglass High were given jobs at Webster High School. A few students helped Conrad Thomas inventory and pack up science equipment and take it to the high school. Then a bulldozer pushed Douglass High School—its walls, its halls, its chairs, and its books—into the basement foundation and covered it with dirt.

The integration of Webster Groves High School went smoothly, except for the fifteen lonely students from Douglass in the class of '57. At Douglass they would have been involved in the choir, the orchestra, the band, football, basketball, or track, and they would have looked forward to dances, concerts, and talent shows. At Webster High School they felt lost and were reluctant to compete. The guidance counselors had never heard of Lincoln University, Fisk University, Howard University, Tuskegee Institute, or Booker T. Washington. It was not until Ronald Woods, a basketball star from North Webster, was elected Webster High School Kampus King in 1961, and Ivory Crockett broke every track record there was in 1968, that black students began to feel they had an important place at Webster Groves High School.

It took longer for other places in Webster Groves to integrate. In the late fifties, when students in the South were staging sit-ins to integrate lunch counters, all of the corner drugstores in Webster Groves removed their soda fountains so that they would not have to face the issue. Because the Toll House Restaurant on Lockwood Avenue refused to serve blacks, the Webster Groves Chapter of CORE picketed outside the restaurant every afternoon and evening until it finally went out of business in 1961.

That same year, Irene Thomas White decided that she wanted to take her three little girls and her son to see Walt Disney's *The Shaggy Dog* at the Ozark Theater in Webster. As they stood in line to buy tickets, it seemed as if the entire Webster Groves police force arrived to ensure that there would not be a disturbance. Benny Gordon and his family also stood in line to see *The Shaggy Dog,* surrounded by police. Gordon talked with the owner of the theater and convinced him that the small-town, family character of the theater would not change if blacks were admitted without police supervision. The owner gave Gordon a date after which blacks would be welcome at the theater. Gordon announced the date at church, and from that time on the Ozark Theater was open to all.

North Webster truly was becoming an integral part of Webster Groves. In 1960 the city of Webster Groves annexed sixty-nine acres of the unincorporated area of North Webster, after the city of Rock Hill had annexed the other unincorporated land between the communities. But it had not been easy. Residents of the unincorporated area, called Webster Heights, had requested annexation by Webster Groves in

1950. Residents of the unincorporated area believed that Webster Groves could provide better police and fire protection than they were receiving from St. Louis County, and better protection would reduce their insurance rates. Annexation would also give Webster Heights sewers, larger water mains for fighting fires, streetlights, and a health code which would prohibit taverns, dumps, and the raising of pigs and chickens. Residents of Webster Heights were already in the Webster Groves School District.

In 1951 the Webster Groves City Plan Commission decided against annexing the unincorporated area because of a report by Harland Bartholomew and Associates, a city planning firm. This report claimed that Webster Heights was not homogeneous in character with the rest of Webster Groves, and that it would cost the city too much to provide public services to the area. The report recommended against annexation. The Webster Groves Interracial Group disputed the report and urged that Webster Heights be annexed. An extensive report by Lee Etta Summytt convinced the League of Women Voters of Webster Groves to favor annexation. The Webster Groves Council of Church Women also favored annexation.

The city council agreed to keep the matter under consideration, and they planned to put it on the ballot in April 1953, along with a $70,000 bond issue to pay for services to the area. But early in 1953 the council decided against including annexation on the ballot, because the swimming pool issue was only just being resolved.

In 1956 the Federal Public Housing Administration approved a St. Louis County Housing Authority slum clearance plan to construct 140 low-rent public-housing units in Webster Heights. The residents of Webster Heights were terrified of what this might mean for their neighborhood, and they again petitioned the city of Webster Groves to annex the unincorporated area. The city council decided against placing annexation on the ballot because of the heavy financial burden it would cause the taxpayers. Luckily, the County Housing Authority plan was held up indefinitely by problems with a similar project in south St. Louis County.

In 1958 the city of Webster Groves created a Land Clearance for Redevelopment Authority so that the city could share the financial burden of urban renewal with the federal government. The LCRA could condemn, purchase, clear, and sell property that had been declared blighted. The federal government required that all displaced residents in an urban renewal project be relocated into standard housing. The LCRA recommended annexation of the unincorporated area and proposed an urban renewal project which would create a forty-acre industrial park on the east side of Kirkham Avenue, on the hill where Pointer's Hall and the Howe Brothers Grocery Store had stood among the trees; a six-acre park on the other side of Kirkham Avenue, where Benny Gordon grew up; and improvement for the twenty-four acres of residential property to the southwest.

In April 1960, the city council put annexation on the ballot, and the voters approved it. Dan Witt and twelve other residents of the annexed area filed suit against the city of Webster Groves, because the residents of the unincorporated area had not been allowed to vote, and many were afraid their houses would be condemned. The case was not decided until 1963, when the St. Louis County Court of Appeals ruled in favor of the city. However, this case influenced the Missouri legislature to pass the Sawyers Act in July 1963, which requires that an area being annexed must vote on the annexation.

In September 1960, urban renewal project Mo. R-15 began in North Webster. In the spring of 1961 the Webster Groves Fire Department burned the 8 worst houses as a training exercise. The city rerouted Shady Creek into a new storm channel to control flooding; improved streets, sidewalks, and street lighting; condemned 83 houses for the new industrial park on Kirkham Avenue and for the new Lorraine Davis Park; rehabilitated 106 houses; built 6 new houses, 2 duplexes, and 2 townhouses; and eliminated all outdoor privies. Mo. R-15 was completed in 1969. Of the eighty-three families who had to relocate, twenty-seven found homes in Webster Groves, twenty found homes in nearby Rock Hill, and the rest moved into St. Louis or elsewhere.

It was difficult to relocate, especially when urban renewal projects were wiping out so many homes in black neighborhoods. In 1964 the city of St. Louis passed a fair-housing ordinance to eliminate racial discrimination in the sale of residential property. A group called Webster Groves Citizens for Fair Housing organized in April 1965 to create an atmosphere of welcome for minorities throughout the community, and to encourage black families to consider all available Webster Groves housing. The group had numerous members, both black and white, and fostered many rewarding interracial friendships. However, it was unable to bring about changes in housing patterns in Webster Groves. The city did not pass a fair-housing ordinance until 1981.

But in the late 1960s, the Webster Groves School Board decided to create that atmosphere of welcome for all children, especially for minorities. At the time of integration, Douglass Elementary School and its faculty had stayed the same. Carl McCree had been the custodian at Douglass for thirty years. He came every morning at 6:00 A.M. to play the piano for an hour or so before he got down to the business of taking care of the school. Howell B. Goins was still the principal. And Elizabeth Winston Walker, who had grown up in North Webster, was the secretary for Douglass High School and Douglass Elementary School from 1946 until the closing of Douglass Elementary in 1978.

In 1967 Goins retired, having been at Douglass forty-one years, thirty-eight years as the principal. In order to better integrate the elementary schools, the Board of Education of Webster Groves asked Henry Givens, a sixth-grade teacher at Douglass, to set up a demonstration school which would be so innovative and so exciting that parents from all over Webster Groves would want to send their children there.

Givens had graduated from Sumner High School in St. Louis, and from Lincoln University in Jefferson City with a degree in elementary education. He had taught fifth and sixth grades at Douglass since 1954.

Givens spent the spring of 1967 working with each of the other principals in the Webster Groves School District, getting to know the faculties, meeting parents, and learning new educational and administrative methods. He spoke to PTAs about the demonstration school and invited teachers from other schools to come to Douglass. He had eighty-five applicants for twenty openings. During the summer of 1967, Givens and the faculty of Douglass created a new curriculum and took out walls at the school to create open classrooms.

Givens grouped grades together, and teachers taught in teams, with two teachers and an aide in each class. Teachers concentrated on their favorite subjects and gave individual attention to each student. Children could read at one grade level and learn math at another level. The Douglass PTA became the largest in the district. Eventually there was a two-year waiting list to get into Douglass.

Douglass was the prototype for a magnet school. In 1970 Henry Givens and Fred Lenhart, a sixth-grade teacher, went to Lima, Peru, to share their teaching ideas. Educators came from all over to observe at Douglass, which had the finest faculty in the nation. The achievement levels of all the children rose. For Henry Givens, "It was a once-in-a-lifetime experience. It was a love affair between a school and a community."

In 1972 Givens left Douglass to become the assistant commissioner of the Missouri State Department of Education, in charge of urban programs. In 1979 he became the president of Harris-Stowe State College.

Ruth Burns became principal of Douglass in 1972. She had taught social studies at the Douglass Demonstration School and at Steger Junior High School. She continued all of the exciting programs of the demonstration school.

In 1978 the Webster Groves School Board had to face a problem which had been approaching for several years. Enrollment was declining, reducing the state and federal funds, which were determined by attendance figures. Inflation was increasing, and the district was almost out of money. Schools had to be closed. A committee of principals, teachers, and parents from all the schools met with the school board, studied the locations, populations, and economics of each school, and recommended that four elementary schools, including Douglass, be closed. The board voted to accept the recommendation. But there was one vote against accepting the recommendation. The president of the Webster Groves School Board, Walter Ambrose, was a 1937 graduate of Douglass High School. Ambrose, a teacher at Vashon High School in St. Louis, was the first black elected to the Webster Groves School Board, and he led the board through its most difficult decision ever.

The end of a good thing is always sad. But as Walter Ambrose said in an interview with high-school students in 1979, "Douglass had always been a great cultural center, steeped in heritage. It was the nucleus of the community for many years. I'm proud of everything that happened back then. But we can't always be looking back or we will stumble. It's time to hold hands and go forward together."

On August 28, 1983, the city of Webster Groves held a dedication ceremony for the Douglass Manor Apartments. Two graduates of Douglass High School, William Thomas, president of the W. A. Thomas Realty Company, and Charles Fleming, president of the Fleming Corporation, a large architectural firm, had converted the school into forty-one apartments and a community room. The two graduates of Douglass gave back to the community some of what Douglass and the community had given to them.

It is fitting to end the story of North Webster with the conversion of the grand old school into something important and dignified with a promising future. The story of North Webster is the story of every black community in America, a tale of segregation and discrimination. Yet North Webster is a special community where excellence was the antidote to discrimination. Because of Douglass, the only accredited high school for blacks in St. Louis County, and because of the community's high aspirations for its youth, individuals from North Webster rose above conditions that held others back.

The outstanding people who have come from Douglass School and North Webster must never be forgotten: William Thomas; Charles Fleming; Walter Ambrose; Eric Donnelly, chief shop steward for the

Mississippi Valley Steel Corporation; Ivory Crockett, at one time the fastest man in the world; Atkins Warren, first black chief of police in Gainesville, Florida, and now regional director of the Department of Justice; Floyd McCree, the first black mayor of Flint, Michigan; Katherine Jane Howell, the first registered nurse to graduate from Lincoln University; James Morrison, who raised prize-winning goats and donated one of his animals to Albert Schweitzer in Africa; John Horner, illustrator for the *Saturday Evening Post;* Ethel Frost, founder of the Missouri Congress of Colored Parents and Teachers; Alphonse Smith, left-fielder for the Cleveland Indians who hit a home run in the 1954 World Series; Buddy Reese, who played trombone in Chicago; Annie Ewing, who taught at Dunbar School for forty-two years; Lewis Bryant, the iceman of North Webster; Joe Thomas, who played the trumpet with Claude Hopkins and Duke Ellington; Harold Esaw, maintenance man for the Missouri Pacific Railroad in charge of the Kirkwood Yard for forty-five years, two months, and nine days; Herbert Witt, Jr., who played tenor saxophone with Lionel Hampton; Winnie Stewart, chief cook for the exclusive Deer Creek Club for twenty-five years; Palmer Goins, chemist at Mallinckrodt Chemical Company; Giles Esaw, the first black policeman in Webster Groves; Margaret Hubbard, director of art for the Detroit Public Schools; Harry Dew, engineer for the city of St. Louis; Paul Witt, who died in the Korean War; Calvin St. James, major in the U.S. Army; Henrietta Ambrose, first black member of the Webster Groves City Council; Benny Gordon, first black realtor in St. Louis County; Benjamin Crockett, certified public accountant in Chicago; Ruby Mitchell Johnson, Women's Army Auxiliary Corps in World War II; DeWitt Davis, Jr., Ph.D. in geography and urban renewal, and professor at the University of the District of Columbia; James Gleason, executive director of the Wabash Avenue YMCA in Chicago and the Harlem YMCA in New York.

"Hail to Douglass, dear old school. Purple and gold, fight on."

REFERENCES

Sources for the Early History of Missouri

1. Anderson, Galusha. *The Story of a Border City during the Civil War*. Boston: Little, Brown and Company, 1908.
2. Eliot, Charlotte C. *William Greenleaf Eliot: Minister, Educator, Philanthropist*. Boston: Houghton, Mifflin and Company, 1904.
3. Scharf, J. Thomas. *History of St. Louis City and County*. Philadelphia: Louis H. Everts and Company, 1883.
4. Violette, Eugene M. *A History of Missouri*. Cape Girardeau, Missouri: Ramfre Press, 1953.
5. Hyde, William, and Conard, Howard. *Encyclopedia of the History of St. Louis*. St. Louis: The Southern History Company, 1899.
6. Green, Lorenzo J.; Kremer, Gary R.; and Holland, Anthony F. *Missouri's Black Heritage*. St. Louis: Forum Press, 1980.
7. Moore, N. Webster. "John Berry Meachum (1789–1854): St. Louis Pioneer, Black Abolitionist, Educator, and Preacher." *Bulletin* 24, no. 2. St. Louis: Missouri Historical Society, 1973.
8. Archives of the St. Louis Mercantile Library Association.
9. Minutes of the Webster Groves Board of Education.
10. Conversations with Marion Jenkins Brooks and Walter Ambrose.

Sources for the History of North Webster through the Civil War

1. Blann, Celeste Wagner. *A History of Rock Hill*. Rock Hill, Missouri: Celeste Wagner Blann, 1976.
2. Start, Clarissa. *Webster Groves*. Webster Groves, Missouri: The City of Webster Groves, 1975.
3. Scharf, J. Thomas. *History of St. Louis City and County*. Philadelphia: Louis H. Everts and Company, 1883.
4. Hyde, William, and Conard, Howard. *Encyclopedia of the History of St. Louis*. St. Louis: The Southern History Company, 1899.
5. Morris, Ann. *The Kate Moody Collection*. St. Louis: Missouri Historical Society, 1983.
6. Morris, Ann. "Reverend Artemas Bullard: Not So Much a Leader as a Product of His Times." Unpublished manuscript, 1981.
7. "Session Minutes of the Rock Hill Presbyterian Church." Rock Hill, Missouri, 1845.
8. "Register of the Rock Hill Presbyterian Church." Rock Hill, Missouri, 1845.
9. Probate Records of James Marshall. St. Louis City Probate Court, 1864.
10. *Vernon's Annotated Missouri Statutes, Under Arrangement of the Official Missouri Revised Statutes*, vol. 24, sec. 451.020. St. Paul, Minnesota: West Publishing Company, 1886.

Sources for the History of North Webster in the 1870s

1. Pitzman, Julius. *An Atlas of St. Louis County*. St. Louis: Julius Pitzman, 1878.
2. Gibson, Capt. Tom L. *Memories of the Old Home Town*. Webster Groves, Missouri: Webster News-Times, 1946.
3. Duncan, R. S. *History of the Baptists in Missouri*. St. Louis: Scammell and Company, 1882.
4. Wallace, Hertha, ed. *The Douglass Oracle, 1935*. Webster Groves, Missouri: Douglass High School, 1935.

5. United States Bureau of the Census. *Central Township, St. Louis, Missouri,* 1870.
6. Morris, Ann. *The Kate Moody Collection.* St. Louis: Missouri Historical Society, 1983.
7. *123rd Anniversary, First Baptist Church.* Webster Groves, Missouri: First Baptist Church, 1989.
8. Minutes of the Webster Groves Board of Education.
9. Evans, Anna Morrison. ''Native Son, Theodore Morrison.'' Unpublished manuscript, 1987.
10. Conversations with Julia Brefford Catlin and Lillian Smith.

Sources for the History of North Webster in the 1880s

1. United States Bureau of the Census. *Central Township, St. Louis, Missouri,* 1880.
2. ''Harold Esaw.'' In *In Retrospect: Webster Groves, Missouri.* Webster Groves, Missouri: Webster Groves High School, 1975.
3. White, Lucy, and Maclin, Yvonne. ''History of Blackwell Chapel, 1884–1984.'' Webster Groves, Missouri: Blackwell Chapel, 1984.
4. Conversations with Harold Esaw, Lucy Esaw Burke, Luther St. James, and Della St. James Brown.

Sources for the History of North Webster in the 1890s

1. ''Harold Esaw.'' In *In Retrospect: Webster Groves, Missouri.* Webster Groves, Missouri: Webster Groves High School, 1975.
2. ''Mrs. Hallie Ewing.'' In *In Retrospect II: Webster Groves, Missouri.* Webster Groves, Missouri: Webster Groves High School, 1976.
3. Wallace, Hertha, ed. *The Douglass Oracle, 1935.* Webster Groves, Missouri: Douglass High School, 1935.
4. Minutes of the Webster Groves Board of Education.
5. Conversations with Harold Esaw, Luther St. James, Annie Gladys Ewing, Hallie Ewing Simpson, and Melzetta Frost Brown.

Sources for the History of North Webster, 1900–1910

1. Wallace, Hertha, ed. *The Douglass Oracle, 1935.* Webster Groves, Missouri: Douglass High School, 1935.
2. Buckner, John D. *History of the Charles Sumner High School, Centennial Edition.* St. Louis: Sumner High School, 1975.
3. ''75th Anniversary, Webster Groves United Methodist Church.'' Webster Groves, Missouri: 75th Anniversary Committee, Webster Groves United Methodist Church, 1983.
4. Evans, Anna Morrison. ''Native Son, Theodore Morrison.'' Unpublished manuscript, 1987.
5. Charter of the Morning Star Lodge, #92. 1880.
6. Conversations with Walter Ambrose, Luther St. James, Harold Esaw, Della St. James Brown, Eric Donnelly, Julia Brefford Catlin, and Melzetta Frost Brown.

Sources for the History of North Webster, 1910–1920

1. *Plat Book of St. Louis County, Missouri.* Des Moines, Iowa: Northwest Publishing Company, 1909.
2. Morris, Ann. *The Kate Moody Collection.* St. Louis: Missouri Historical Society, 1983.
3. ''Parks Chapel Historical Sketch.'' Webster Groves, Missouri: Parks Chapel, 1969.
4. Evans, Anna Morrison. ''Native Son, Theodore Morrison.'' Unpublished manuscript, 1987.
5. Minutes of the Webster Groves Board of Education.
6. ''What Our Negro Soldiers Did in the Great War.'' St. Louis *Post Dispatch,* February 16, 1919.
7. Conversations with Della St. James Brown, Rosalee Shepard, Walter Ambrose, Luther St. James, and Marion Jenkins Brooks.

Sources for the History of North Webster in the 1920s

1. Primm, James Neal. *Lion of the Valley: St. Louis, Missouri.* Boulder, Colorado: Pruett Publishing Company, 1981.
2. Anderson, Jervis. *This Was Harlem.* New York: Farrar Straus Giroux, 1981.
3. Morris, Ann. *The Kate Moody Collection.* St. Louis: Missouri Historical Society, 1983.
4. Mitchell, Edwina W. *The Crusading Black Journalist: Joseph Everett Mitchell.* St. Louis: Farmer Press, Inc., 1972.
5. *Plat Book of St. Louis County, Missouri.* Des Moines, Iowa: Northwest Publishing Company, 1909.
6. Wallace, Hertha, ed. *The Douglass Oracle, 1935.* Webster Groves, Missouri: Douglass High School, 1935.
7. *123rd Anniversary, First Baptist Church.* Webster Groves, Missouri: First Baptist Church, 1989.
8. "History of Nazarene Baptist Church." In *Our 65th Church Anniversary.* Webster Groves, Missouri: Nazarene Baptist Church, 1989.
9. Wyatt, Imelda Thomas. "Memories." Unpublished manuscript, 1987.
10. Nevels, Lucy Witt. "Witt Family, 1921 to 1987." Unpublished manuscript, 1987.
11. Catlin, Julia Brefford. "A History of Rogers Ice Cream Parlor." Unpublished manuscript, 1987.
12. Minutes of the Webster Groves Board of Education.
13. Young, Hallie. "Roscoe James." Unpublished manuscript, 1987.
14. Kennedy, Hallister. Oral History Interview by Doris Wesley, April 27, 1990. Western Historical Manuscript Collection, University of Missouri–St. Louis.
15. Conversations with Ruby Mitchell Johnson, Mildred Miles Cole, Walter Ambrose, Harold Schaeffer, Julia Brefford Catlin, Anna Morrison Evans, Ted Yandell, Jr., Roscoe James, Carol Thomas Johnson, Conrad Thomas, Melzetta Frost Brown, Harold Esaw, Hallie Ewing Simpson, Eric Donnelly, Lee Etta Summytt, Hutcher Dixon, and Jewel Tappel.
16. Webster Groves City Ordinance #3807, Changing the Name of Shady Avenue; May 1929.

Sources for the History of North Webster in the 1930s

1. Anderson, Jervis. *This Was Harlem.* New York: Farrar Straus Giroux, 1981.
2. Reichler, Joseph. *The Baseball Encyclopedia.* 6th ed. New York: Macmillan, 1985.
3. "Webster Groves's Last GAR Survivor Is a Former Slave." *Webster News-Times,* August 5, 1932.
4. Minutes of the Webster Groves Board of Education.
5. Conversations with Henry St. James, Frank Witt, Annie Gladys Ewing, Benny Gordon, Walter Pierpont Ewing, Hutcher Dixon, and the North Central Association Commission on Schools.
6. Goins, H. B. Oral History Interview, Spring 1979, Webster Groves Historical Society Archives.
7. Radford, Edward L. "Implementing Court-ordered Desegregation for the Ferguson Reorganized School District R2: A Case Study." Ph.D. dissertation, St. Louis University, 1979.

Sources for the History of North Webster in the 1940s

1. Mitchell, Edwina W. *The Crusading Black Journalist: Joseph Everett Mitchell.* St. Louis: Farmer Press, Inc., 1972.
2. Weigley, Russel F. *Eisenhower's Lieutenants.* Bloomington: Indiana University Press, 1981.
3. Wilmot, Chester. *The Struggle for Europe.* London: Collins, 1952.
4. David, Lester. "Gangway for the Red Ball Express." *American Legion,* January 1984.
5. Williams, James D., and Branch, Kip. "Tuskegee Airmen." *Crisis,* June/July 1991.
6. Minutes of the Webster Groves Board of Education.
7. "Old Community Baptist Church: 1866–1945–1986." Webster Groves, Missouri: Old Community Baptist Church, 1986.
8. Gill, Robert L. "The Spiritual and Monumental Legacy of a Civil Rights Lawyer." *Journal of Human Relations* 16 (1968).
9. Conversations with Roscoe James, Walter Ambrose, Carol Thomas Johnson, Melzetta Frost Brown, Imelda Thomas Wyatt, Conrad Thomas, Hutcher Dixon, and Benny Gordon.

Sources for the History of North Webster in the 1950s

1. Primm, James Neal. *Lion of the Valley: St. Louis, Missouri.* Boulder, Colorado: Pruett Publishing Company, 1981.
2. Records of the Webster Groves League of Women Voters, Webster Groves Historical Society Archives.
3. Records of the United Church Women of Webster Groves, Webster Groves Historical Society Archives.
4. *Witt, Frank, vs. Wood, Ray, et al.* St. Louis County Circuit Court, May 29, 1950.
5. Minutes of the Webster Groves City Council, 1950, 1951, 1952, 1953.
6. *Souvenir Album: 10th Anniversary of the Women's Achievement Association.* St. Louis: Achievement House, 1957.
7. *Webster News-Times,* 1951–1953.
8. Wyatt, Imelda Thomas. ''Memories.'' Unpublished manuscript, 1987.
9. Dedication Ceremony for Walter Rusan Field, in Files at Webster Groves Board of Education.
10. Conversations with Benny Gordon; Judge Theodore McMillian; Paul Saunders, Professor of Law at Vanderbilt University; Walter Ambrose; Eugene Wehrli, President of Eden Theological Seminary; Allan Miller, Professor of Theology at Eden Theological Seminary; Carol Thomas Johnson; the Reverend Benjamin Catlin; the Reverend Charles and Dorothy Rehkopf; Congressman Thomas B. Curtis; Irene Thomas White; Conrad Thomas; and Martha Hill.

Sources for the History of North Webster in the 1960s

1. *The Echo.* Webster Groves High School Yearbook, 1961.
2. Records of the Webster Groves League of Women Voters, Webster Groves Historical Society Archives.
3. Greater St. Louis Committee for Freedom of Residence Records, Western Historical Manuscript Collection, University of Missouri–St. Louis.
4. *Webster Advertiser,* February 1960–May 1965.
5. Start, Clarissa. ''Somehow All 9 Children Got to College.'' St. Louis *Post Dispatch*, July 13, 1962.
6. Webster Groves Fair Housing Ordinance, 1981.
7. Conversations with Coach Bob Hoffmann, Irene Thomas White, Benny and Lorraine Gordon, Walter Ambrose, Webster Groves City Attorney Allen Boston, Henry St. James, Carol Thomas Johnson, and Dr. Henry Givens.

Sources for the History of North Webster in the 1970s

1. Report and Recommendations of the Webster Groves School District Economics Committee to the Board of Education. February 1978.
2. Ambrose, Walter. Oral History Interview, Spring 1979, Webster Groves Historical Society Archives.
3. Conversations with Dr. Henry Givens, Dr. Max Wolfrum, William A. Thomas, Miriam Thomas Berry, Irene Thomas White, Ruth Thomas Banks, and Alice Thomas Ware.

Fairfax, built in 1839 by James C. Marshall for his wife, Elizabeth McCausland Marshall. Marshall moved to St. Louis from Fairfax, Virginia, in 1832 with his brother, John, and their slaves. With their trading post close by, Fairfax became a stopping place for the State Stage Line from St. Louis to Kansas City. It was also the first post office in the area. Mail was picked up and delivered three times a week.

Ed Purnell, a former slave of James Marshall, in front of the log cabin built by his father, John Purnell, on Litzinger Road.

Allen Brown and his wife, Julia, came to Webster Groves from Alabama in 1866 with a wagon and a mule given to him by his former master.

56   Mary Brown Brefford, daughter of Allen Brown, was a member of the first class to
graduate from the eighth grade at Douglass School, in 1898.

Arnold Brown, son of Allen Brown. Arnold and his older sister, Mary, were members of the first class to graduate from the eighth grade at Douglass School, in 1898.

58   George Brown, son of Allen Brown, ran away from home at a young age to fight in the Spanish-American War.

Allen Brefford in front of Grandfather Allen Brown's house at 66 Lincoln Avenue.

Eleanor Brown Rogers, daughter of Allen and Julia Brown.

Preston Rogers, 1914. Rogers married Eleanor Brown. They operated an ice cream parlor next to their home on North Elm.

Eleanor and Preston Rogers and friends in front of the Rogers house, 540 North Elm Avenue, in 1915.

Forty morning worshipers in front of First Baptist Church before the turn of the century. Organized in 1866, First Baptist Church is one of the oldest churches in Webster Groves.

The Shepperd family on the way to church, around 1900.

The Shepperd family about 1916.

The Casey family. They came to Webster Groves from Augusta, Missouri, in 1908.

Annie Polk took in boarders, usually teachers from Douglass School. Polk Avenue was named for her.

68   Lucy Esaw Burks, age 8. Her father, Jacob Esaw, came to Webster Groves from Searcy, Arkansas, around 1880.

Harold Esaw, shown here at age 7, worked for the Missouri Pacific Railroad for 45 years, 2 months, and 9 days.

Giles Esaw, shown here at age 14, grew up to be a policeman.

Blackwell Chapel on Shady Avenue, in 1892. The Reverend J. B. Bunch was pastor.

Mrs. Anna Amelia Morrison and her son, Robert, in 1878. Anna and her husband, John Anderson Morrison, came to Webster Groves from Searcy, Arkansas, around 1870.

72   The Reverend Theodore Morrison, first pastor of Parks Chapel A.M.E. Church.

Fiftieth wedding anniversary of the Reverend and Mrs. Theodore Morrison, August 1955.

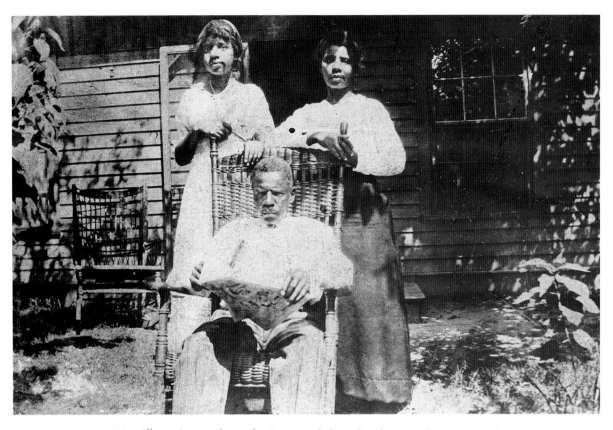

Mr. Albert Givens, his wife, Rose, and their daughter, Helen, at 148 Slocum, about 1915.

Helen Givens, 1920.

Sarah Givens at 148 Slocum, about 1920.

Martha Stone came to Webster Groves in 1893 so that her children could get a good education.

Frank Stone lived on Fox Place. In 1917 he and Augustus Ewing of Webster Groves and Mr. and Mrs. William Jenkins of Kirkwood went to the Missouri Supreme Court seeking a high-school education for all black children in Missouri.

Hugh Stone, Frank Stone's only son, served in World War I.

80   Ethel Stone Frost, daughter of Frank and Martha Stone, helped to organize the Missouri Branch of the National Congress of Colored Parents and Teachers in 1927.

Frank Stone's daughters. *Front row:* Victoria Shelton, Beulah Futrell; *second row:* Deli-
lah Turnley, Molly Isom, Ethel Frost, Josephine Van Winkle; *third row:* Elizabeth
Weaver, Maude Futrell.

82   A. D. Pierson came to Webster Groves in 1893. Pierson was the community's first
black concrete engineer, and he built the first septic tanks in Webster Groves.

Hallie Katherine Pierson Ewing as a student at George R. Smith University around 1900. The Ewings operated a well-known dairy farm on Lithia Avenue and Rock Hill Road for many years.

The Ewing children around 1911: Augustus P., Annie, Walter Pierpont, Sarah, and Benjamin.

The Harden boys, Louis, Bill, and Richard, around 1916.

Douglass School on Holland Avenue in the late 1920s. This building began as a two-room frame school serving grades one through eight in 1892. Basement rooms were added in 1913, and three rooms were added in 1925 to create a "High School Department."

The teachers of Douglass School around 1920. *Standing:* Laura Nichollson and Susie Lewis; *seated:* Principal Thomas A. Moore and Harvey Simms.

Douglass Grade School, fifth and sixth grades, 1922. Professor Harvey Simms is standing at top left.

The eighth-grade graduating class of Douglass School, 1924. Principal Thomas A. Moore is seated.

The teachers of Douglass School, 1924-1925. *Standing:* Harvey Simms, Susie Lewis, and Principal Thomas A. Moore; *seated:* Marguerite Parker, Ada Clark, Edith Rhetta, and Nellie Salmon.

90

The eighth-grade graduating class of Douglass School, 1925. Principal Thomas A. Moore is seated.

Herbert G. Witt, Sr., and his wife, Lucy Criddle Witt, on their wedding day, June 15, 1916.

James and Lucy Sweezer, 1920.

The Douglass School Band, directed by Harvey Simms, with visiting instructor P. B. Lankford, around 1920. Joe Thomas, ninth from the left, went on to play the trumpet with Claude Hopkins and Duke Ellington. Buddy Reese, fifth from the right, later played the trombone in Chicago.

96   Mrs. Lee Etta Summytt, before World War I. Mrs. Summytt's husband, Elvis, was a pharmacist and operated the only drugstore in North Webster. The Summytts had no children of their own, but they adopted five, putting all of them through school.

William C. Reed, World War I.

98 Andrew Evans lived on North Elm. Evans was freed by the Emancipation Proclamation when he was 18 years old. He joined the Union Army in Illinois, and in 1932 he was the last survivor of the Civil War living in Webster Groves. He learned to read when he was 70.

Mr. Andrew Thomas. He commuted on the train every day to St. Louis, where he worked at a candy company.

Mrs. Miriam Thomas loved to cook. Every Sunday she had company from the Central Baptist Church in St. Louis for dinner.

The home of Andrew and Miriam Thomas on Taylor (now called Thornton), soon after they moved to Webster Groves in 1915. The house was built of rock from a nearby quarry.

Mrs. Alby Thomas, daughter-in-law of Andrew and Miriam Thomas, about 1918.

The Thomas grocery store and cleaning establishment on North Elm Avenue, late 1930s. The Charles Thomas family lived next door to their store.

The Charles Thomas family. *Standing:* William, Irene, Consuella, Miriam, Ruth, Imelda, Alice, and Clarence; *seated:* Mae, Mrs. Alby Thomas, Mr. Charles Thomas, and Mr. Thomas's sister, Alice.

The Webster Groves Methodist Episcopal Church, on top of the hill on Cornell Avenue. This church was torn down in 1979 when a new church building was erected next door. The church changed its name to Webster Groves United Methodist Church in 1968. In 1989 it merged with St. Mark's Methodist Episcopal Church of Richmond Heights, and the name was changed to Unity United Methodist Church of Webster Groves.

The Carl Walker family, around 1916. Carl Walker was an enthusiastic follower of Marcus Garvey.

The Webster Reds baseball team, which played in the Bottoms. Joe Turner, owner of the Vendome (a nightclub), coached the Webster Reds.

The hearse of the J. C. Lewis Funeral Home at the Father Dickson Cemetery, 1928. Lewis's motto was "Our telephone never sleeps."

J. C. and Susie Lewis having fun in their new 1922 Ford.

Four boys on a birdwatching field trip from Douglass School, around 1915. Second from the left is Luther St. James, third is George Clark, and fourth is Elmer Carter.

Douglass High School football team, 1928.

MAYDA MORGAN. LOUIS MARDEN. HELEN MORTON.

DAVID HAWKINS. RORBERT THOMAS.

CLASS DOUGLASS. HIGH. SCHOOL. 1929.

HILDRED CAMPBELL. IMELDA THOMAS.

MATTYE GILL. S. SUPT H.S. DAVIS. A.B. RINEHART THELMA WEEKS.

112   The first graduating class from Douglass High School, 1929. Principal Herbert S. Davis is at bottom center.

Howell B. Goins, soon after he became principal of Douglass Elementary, Junior High, and High School in 1929. Goins served as principal for 38 years.

Harvey J. Simms, who became a teacher at Douglass School in 1916. Although he walked with a crutch, he played football and coached baseball. He directed the first Douglass School Band for 10 years. He served as the clerk of the Old Community Baptist Church. Simms wrote a society column for the *St. Louis Argus,* and he wrote more than 100 obituaries, many before the subjects were deceased.

Harvey Simms in his first automobile, 1920.

116   Sarah Simms Wright on a trip east with the Beardsley family of Webster, for whom she worked.

Sarah Simms Wright in the 1930s. She had dated Scott Joplin in her youth.

The Simms home on Shady Avenue, now called Kirkham Avenue.

Reunion of Etta Simms and her family in 1937, in front of her home at 450 West Kirkham.

Thenia Middlebrooks in front of the old Frazier-Phelps homestead on Thornton Avenue, which later burned. The car is an old Studebaker.

Julia Mae Clark on Shady Avenue after graduating from nurses' training, 1929.

Three sisters, Maggie, Pauline, and Clara, about 1920.

First Baptist Church in the new building at 159 East Kirkham in the late 1920s.

Mrs. Annie Gordon Blackburn with her sons Benny and Edward Gordon, 1929.

Three generations: Benny Gordon, first black realtor in St. Louis County; Marvin Gordon, real-estate appraiser; and Marvin Gordon, Jr.

A CCC camp in Missouri during the Great Depression. John Blackburn is the second from the left.

Deer Creek floodwaters at Kirkham and Wellington. After every big rain, the last families out had to be evacuated in Red Cross boats.

Lonzella Wallace Rogers and Mamie Johnson McCall standing in floodwaters of Deer Creek at Kirkham and Wellington, early 1940s.

Floodwaters of Deer Creek, looking south from Brentwood Boulevard to Kirkham at Wellington.

Kirkwood-Ferguson streetcars backed up by floodwaters on Kirkham Avenue in the 1930s.

WPA project to control flooding along Deer Creek, next to Marshall Avenue. Deer Creek is a tributary of River Des Peres.

Dr. Eric C. Donnelly, standing on the porch of his home and office at 239 East Kirkham. He came to Webster Groves about 1928 and was one of two black doctors who practiced in the community. He died in 1946.

Ida Mae Donnelly, wife of Dr. Eric C. Donnelly. Their son, Eric C. Donnelly, Jr., became the chief shop steward of Mississippi Valley Steel Corporation.

134   Leon Houston on a swing behind the Walter C. Haussler home, 5767 Lindell Boulevard, in the 1930s. Houston was a butler and chauffeur for the Haussler family for more than fifty years.

The Chauffeurs and Butlers Club of St. Louis in the 1930s. Leon Houston is in the front row, far right.

136 Allie Mae Bryant and Lewis Bryant, Jr., 1929.

Lewis Bryant, Sr., the iceman of Webster Groves, 1935. He was a charter member of the North Webster Firefighters Association and helped build the firehouse on Bell Avenue.

North Webster Volunteer Firefighters, 1941. *Top row:* E. Reid, S. Bowman, T. Crenshaw, R. Atchison, and J. Ewing. *Bottom row:* A. Spears, C. Harris, W. Dixon, H. Reid, and C. Dixon.

North Webster Volunteer Firefighters Association Annual Dinner at Douglass High School, 1940s.

Inside the Vendome nightclub in the 1930s. The Vendome was located in the Bottoms, just north of where Lorraine Davis Park is today.

The Regal Singers: Ranken Esaw, Barnett Reeves, William Franklin, Cornelius Walker, and Edward Reeves, 1939.

Douglass senior class of 1935.

Cub Scouts in the 1930s: Elmer Phelps, James Hinkle, and Theodore McGinnis.

Edith McCree, Cynthia (Sudy) Taylor, and Myrtle Morrison in front of Blackwell Chapel on North Elm in the late 1930s.

A Douglass class in the 1930s.

Douglass students, proud of their history display.

Three friends at Douglass School.

A cigar-box project in the early 1940s.

Douglass School in the 1940s. Douglass served elementary and junior high-school students from Webster Groves, and high-school students from all over St. Louis County and as far away as Washington, Missouri.

Walter L. Ambrose, Douglass High School class of 1937.

Walter Ambrose graduated from Douglass School in 1937 and from Lincoln University in 1941. He served as an aide to General George S. Patton during World War II. He earned a master's degree in education from St. Louis University, then taught in the St. Louis public schools for 41 years. Ambrose was the first black member of the Webster Groves Board of Education, serving for 12 years. He was president of the board 1977-78, during the very difficult year when Douglass Elementary School had to be closed.

Mrs. Harriet Ashcraft in front of her home on Holland. Mrs. Ashcraft taught fourth grade at Douglass and led a Brownie troop after school.

The St. James cow, across the street from two of the St. James houses at the top of Holland Avenue.

Mattie Wilkins and her children, Rose and David. Mrs. Wilkins was a widow and an active member and strong supporter of First Baptist Church. During the week she worked tirelessly for the First Congregational Church of Webster Groves.

William Dixon, owner of Dixon's grocery, and his mother, affectionately called "Grandma Dixon."

Dixon's store on Waymire in the early 1950s.

Hutcher Dixon, about 17 years old, before entering World War II.

Sarah and Henry Lewis. Sarah had a beauty shop on North Elm.

Henry Lewis, private barber to August A. Busch.

Old Community Baptist Church in the 1940s.

O.D.T. (Our Day Together) Club members: Arilla Spears, Lorraine Davis, Susie Lewis, Ida Phelps, and Augusta Boulding. O.D.T. is a women's club which was organized in Webster Groves in the 1930s to provide scholarships and encourage neighborhood beautification and other civic projects.

Mrs. Mildred Lipscomb at her home on Wellington (called Waymire today). When her daughter, Jeanette Gleason, died in 1940, just before graduating from Lincoln University, Mrs. Lipscomb established the Jeanette Gleason Scholarship Fund, which helped many Douglass students go to college.

162

Mary McElroy Hall, whose grandparents were born in Webster Groves and helped organize Blackwell Chapel.

163

164   A group of Douglass High School majorettes showing off their new uniforms. The girls paid for their own uniforms.

Douglass High School graduation, 1944. Arthur Hinch is in uniform in the center.

166   Arthur Hinch, drafted along with many other boys from Douglass two months before
he would have graduated in 1944. He came back on leave to graduate.

Gale Wilkinson and his buddies at army camp during World War II. **167**

168   Anthony Billinger, France, 1945. Billinger was a graduate of Douglass School.

Clyde Wallace in Paris, France, 1945.

170   Sergeant Ruby Mitchell Johnson served in the Women's Army Auxiliary Corps from February 18, 1943, to December 7, 1946; Fourth Air Force, Walla Walla, Washington, 423rd Base Unit.

Welcome Home Banquet for soldiers of World War II, Douglass High School gym,
March 31, 1946.

Sisters Clentery and Otessa Franks.

Cousins Mack Davis, Clentery Franks, Otessa Franks, Georgia Davis, and Ezekiel Davis. **173**

174   W. P. Brown in "civvies" after returning home from World War II.

James Goolsby and Wardie Hall, after World War II.

Doris Jean Whittaker Ellis, about 1945.

Henrietta Smith Ambrose, 1943. In 1986 she became the first black member of the City Council of Webster Groves.

Mrs. Eliza Smith in front of her home on Kirkham Avenue, around 1945.

Teen Town at Douglass School, around 1940.

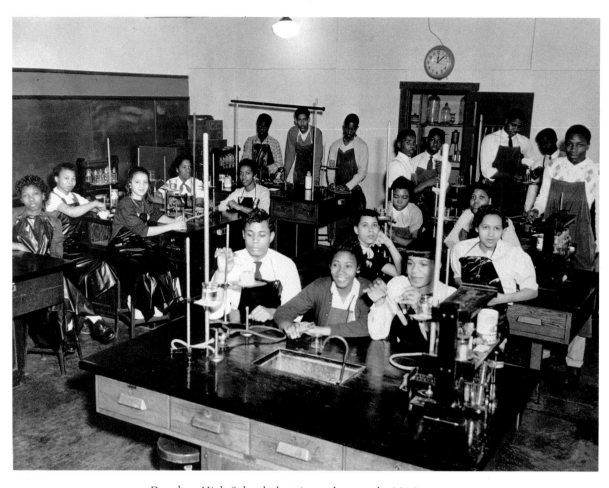

Douglass High School chemistry class, early 1950s.

Mr. and Mrs. Walter Rusan and their two sons. For many years Walter Rusan was the president of the Douglass PTA. In 1944 he organized the North Webster YMCA. Rusan spent most of his life promoting interracial cooperation.

182   Lucille (Mrs. Walter) Rusan.

A group of friends at a Douglass High School picnic in the 1940s. The boys are
Donald Rusan and Ralph Smith; the girls are Mamie Johnson McCall, Martha Jean
Hall Rusan, and Elizabeth Winston Walker.

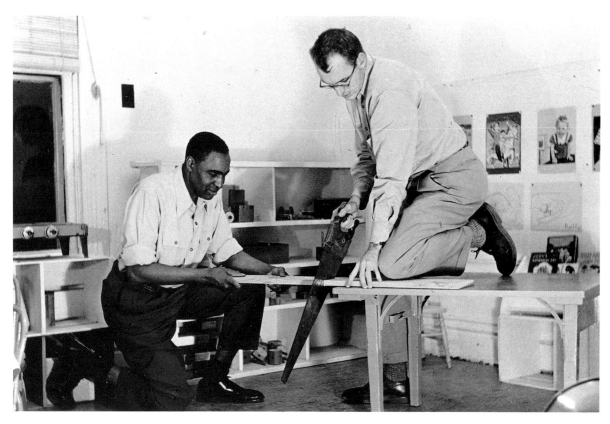

Walter Rusan and Philip Gale working at the Nellie Salmon Nursery School. Mrs. Salmon bequeathed her home to be used as an interracial nursery school after her death in 1950.

Charles Hall in 1950 with the Brooklyn Dodgers' Farm Club, Elmira, New York. In 1949 he played with the Kansas City Monarchs before becoming the property of the Brooklyn Dodgers.

Paul Witt gave his life in the Korean War.

James McCall, Solomon Wilson, Moses Jenkins, and Dorsey Jessup in front of Piggy's Pool Hall and the Bobbit property on North Elm.

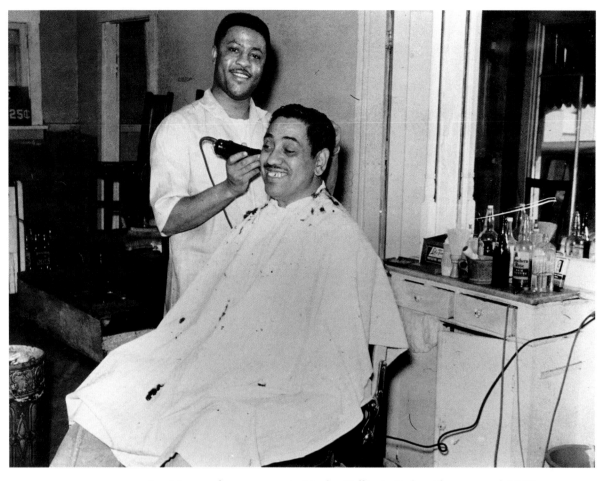

Lee Moss and a customer in Mosby Collins's Barber Shop around 1960.

Henry Givens was the principal of Douglass Elementary School from 1967 until 1972. He established an exciting, innovative demonstration school which became a model for magnet schools. Today Givens is the president of Harris-Stowe State College.

Lawson Buford joined the Webster Groves Police Department in June 1968 and rose to the rank of sergeant.

James Morrison with prize-winning Nubian goat at the Illinois State Fair. He operated the Elm Hills Farm on North Elm in Webster Groves until his death in 1989. In 1957 Morrison was one of eight dairy goat breeders to donate animals to Dr. Albert Schweitzer to produce milk for Dr. Schweitzer's hospital in Africa.

Wedding party of Peggy and Lorenzo Jones at the home of the bride's parents, Mr. and Mrs. William Rogers, 502 North Elm, in 1952.

ANN MORRIS is associate director of the Western Historical Manuscript Collection at the University of Missouri–St. Louis. She has written numerous articles on history for the *Webster-Kirkwood Times.*

HENRIETTA AMBROSE grew up in North Webster, served as president of the Webster Groves Historical Society, and is the first black person elected to the Webster Groves City Council.

JOHN NAGEL is Associate Professor of Photography at St. Louis Community College at Meramec.

JULIUS K. HUNTER, a native of St. Louis, is a veteran television news anchor, author, historian, lecturer, and teacher.